BACKYARD
MOSAICS

BACKYARD
MOSAICS

Connie Sheerin

Sterling Publishing Co., Inc.
New York

Prolific Impressions Production Staff:

Editor: Mickey Baskett
Copy: Phyllis Mueller
Graphics: Dianne Miller, Karen Turpin
Photography: Pat Molnar
Administration: Jim Baskett

Library of Congress Cataloging-in-Publication Data

Sheerin, Connie.
    Backyard mosaics / Connie Sheerin.
       p. cm.
    ISBN 0-8069-2967-7 Hardcover
    ISBN 1-4027-0106-3 Paperback
       1. Garden ornaments and furniture. 2. Mosaics. I. Title.

    SB473.5 .S54 2001
    717--dc21

                                                    2001020913

10 9 8 7 6 5 4 3 2
First paperback edition published in 2002 by
Sterling Publishing Company, Inc.
387 Park Avenue South, New York, N.Y. 10016
Produced by Prolific Impressions, Inc.
160 South Candler St., Decatur, GA 30030
©2001 by Prolific Impressions, Inc.
Distributed in Canada by Sterling Publishing
ᶜ/o Canadian Manda Group, One Atlantic Avenue, Suite 105
Toronto, Ontario, Canada M6K 3E7
Distributed in Australia by Capricorn Link (Australia) Pty. Ltd.
P.O. Box 704, Winsdor, NSW 2756 Australia
Printed in China
All rights reserved
Sterling ISBN 0-8069-2967-7 Hardcover
        ISBN 1-4027-0106-3 Paperback

Acknowledgments

The designer wishes to thank the companies that contributed products for use in the projects:

For uniquely shaped tiles, glass pieces, vintage china tiles, inspirational tiles, relief tiles, wood tiles, mirror tiles, colored grout, tile nippers, and glass cutters:
Crafts ala Cart
1612 Union Valley Road
West Milford, New Jersey 07480
973-657-1612
www.craftsalacart.com

For grout and grout sealer:
Custom Building Products
Polyblend
13001 Seal Beach Blvd.
Seal Beach, CA 90740
1-800-272-8786

For Make-It Mosaic® products, FolkArt® Acrylic Colors, Apple Barrel Colors® and Durable Colors™ paints, and self-adhesive foil tape:
Plaid Enterprises, Inc.
P.O. Box 7600
Norcross, GA 30091-7600
www.plaidonline.com

For adhesives:
Beacon Adhesives
125 MacQuesten Pkwy. S.
Mount Vernon, NY 10550
www.beaconcreates.com

For unique shapes and raised tiles:
Orlandini Tile Co.
Walnut & Pine St.
Marcus Hook, PA 19061

Dedication

*This book is dedicated to my mother, **Virginia Fischer,** who continues to support me in my creative endeavors, as she has done my entire life, and to my father, Ted Fischer, who I am sure is in heaven selling advance copies!*

Special Thanks

When my first book on mosaics, *Mosaics in an Afternoon,* was published and I was receiving so many compliments, I realized it needs to be said that no book comes together without the help of many talented people. It takes a mosaic of people to bring a book to fruition.

This is my second book with my editor, **Mickey Baskett,** who certainly knows, better than anyone, how to take my finished pieces and put them in settings that show them at their very best. She has patience and understanding and shows great persistence in moving me along. The creative part is the easy for me. Sitting at the computer to write the instructions takes discipline. Thank you, Mickey, for moving – sometimes pushing – me along.

Because I have watched so many of my students grow in their creativity, I invited some of them to add their creative pieces to this book. For their outstanding contributions, I thank **Robyn Huber, Carla D'Iorio, and Dolly Clark.**

And then there is the girls' club that came to the studio to help execute the designs I created, often adding a touch or two of their own. Not only did they grout, nip, paint and glue, but they added so much fun on the late nights as we sang to the oldies, had a glass of wine or two, and chatted and laughed while we all worked – much like the quilting bees of yesterday. For their help and support, I thank **Danielle Franklin Bruno, Dana Clark, Ann Rogers, and Dolly Clark.**

The thanks would not be complete if I did not thank all of my friends from my **Women's Joy Group** for their continuing support and for their understanding of my missing several meetings this year. It has been a very busy time, and it is so wonderful knowing that they and all of my wonderful girlfriends are out there wishing me well.

I also thank my partners in **Crafts ala Cart** who pitched in and did my work when I was working on my book. I have never heard a word of complaint, although they may have had something to say when I was not listening! (Only kidding, gals!)

I thank **Alicia,** my daughter, for always telling me I can do it and more! She is one of my best cheerleaders and uses her public relations and marketing talents to talk about her mom's endeavors whenever she can!

And then there is my sweet little **Angel** dog, who sits with me way into the early hours of the morning while I am alone in the studio creating. I never feel alone when she is by my side all snug in her little doggie bed. You can see her sweet face as she sits in a basket on the chair in the garden.

It was a hot August day when we photographed this chair. Before we knew it, my editor had Angel in the basket. Although panting in the August heat, the picture turned out great! So did the chair! See page 92 for instructions.

And last – but certainly not least – I thank my wonderful husband, **Ken Williams,** who bought me a laptop computer so I can write whenever and wherever the spirit moves me. I also thank him for eating lots of takeout food and soup on the many nights I am not around to be Betty Crocker. (Not that I have ever been much at that anyway!) Most of all, I thank him for his unconditional love and support in my creative pursuits.

For each of the pieces that my friends and colleagues have brought to this book, I humbly thank them.

Always creating something,
Connie Sheerin

About the Artist

Connie Sheerin

Connie Sheerin has crafted in one way or another for as long as she can remember. Although she majored in communications, she earned spending money in college doing pastel portraits of her friends.

While looking for her first real job, she took a night school class in crafts. The instructor, who owned a small craft shop, was looking for a manager, and hired Connie. Connie stayed in the crafts industry – designing, demonstrating, and teaching – until her daughter, Alicia, was born. Wanting to be a stay-at-home mom, Connie staged in-home craft parties, ran holiday craft sales at her home, and sold her design work to different manufacturers.

After she divorced, Connie wanted to be with her daughter as much as possible, so she began a program called Crafts ala Cart, an in-patient crafts program in 10 area hospitals. She and several friends then opened a retail store, Crafts ala Cart Studio, offering an array of crafts supplies and classes.

During that time, Connie began doing live TV in the Philadelphia area as the Crafts Lady, bringing viewers a new craft each week. Eventually, she was producing, directing, and starring in five-minute craft segments called "Connie's Craft Quickies," which she marketed to over 50 television stations throughout the country.

Recently she has been a guest demonstrator on numerous television programs, including *The Rosie O'Donnell Show*, *The Carol Duvall Show*, *Home Matters*, *Handmade by Design*, and *Willard Scott's Farm & Garden Journal*.

After spending 10 years working in public relations and marketing special events, Connie tired of the fast pace and traveling and returned to the craft industry in 1995. Today, she designs, writes, and has resurrected Crafts ala Cart, which is now a multi-level at-home workshop business she formed with three partners that gives creative women a chance to teach while developing their marketing and business skills.

One of her favorite crafts is mosaics, and she is the author of *Mosaics in an Afternoon* (Sterling, 1999). Her project book, *Creative Mosaics*, was published by Plaid Enterprises in 1998. She is a member of the Society of Craft Designers and the Society of American Mosaic Artists.

Connie resides in Lansdowne, Pennsylvania with her husband Ken Williams, a therapist who works with adolescents, and her studio sidekick, Angel, a teacup yorkie. "Life is good," Connie says. "I am blessed to be able to work at what I really love – turning my dreams into creative realities." ❏

Contents

Introduction

If I'd had a crystal ball instead of a mosaic bowling ball, I might have been able to predict the future and my second book on mosaics. I would have never thrown out a broken dish, piece of pottery, or knick-knack or old piece of furniture. And I would have spent more time on bulk trash day picking more trash to make into mosaic treasures.

Of course, it's good that we don't own crystal balls and know everything that our future will bring because, as crafters, we would have to own a second home just to save our stuff. And as loving and supportive as the good husband is, my craft things have managed to invade every room in our home. If you have read this far, you are right on my wavelength and will understand and, hopefully, enjoy the stories of how many of these pieces came to be. It has been a fun – and often very funny – journey.

When my editor called and asked if I would like to do a book on backyard mosaics, I was very happy but thought that it could be limiting. Ha! Was I surprised. Just you wait until you begin to look for items that will be just right for your garden, your backyard, your porch, your deck, or your pond (if you are one of those lucky folks who has one in your backyard to meditate by). Oh, how happy a little mosaic Buddha or frog looks next to a fish pond! You will find both and more on the beautifully photographed pages of this book.

Finding locations for shooting was fun for me too. I hope these pictures will inspire you to think of spots for mosaic pieces in your backyard. I thank the Huber-Walkers and the Whiteheads for the use of their lovely properties.

If you, like me, live in a cold climate, you may want to bring some of your mosaic creations inside to enjoy for the winter months (and to protect them so you won't have to do repairs in the spring). Pieces of furniture should at least be covered, just as you cover other outdoor furniture during months of more severe weather.

• Recent Mosaic History

Many wonderful books written on mosaics in the past few years have more than covered the long history of mosaics so I thought it might be interesting to write a bit about the recent resurgence of this ancient art.

Mosaics are truly experiencing a renaissance. Artisans are stretching their imaginations using bits and pieces of all kinds of materials, including tiles, china, glass, pottery pieces, buttons, shells, and stones – collectively called "tesserae" – giving everyone with a creative bent towards mosaics the ability to enjoy it within their budget. Everything you use to create a mosaic can be a recycled item, from the surface you work on to the tesserae you cover the piece with. There are tiles that cost as much as $50 each, but you can find tiles of great interest and value at yard sales, swaps, and secondhand shops for a pittance. Sometimes you will find just one tile that will begin the creation of a new piece – a new idea – and you will build around it. Keep your eyes open; you will be surprised at what may spark your imagination and be the start of your next mosaic.

Working on this book has sent me on a mission to find unusual materials and hopefully you will be inspired to do the same. Feel free to contact me – I can guide you as to where to buy the unusual. I would also love to hear from any of you who find unusual items so I can share them through e-mail with my readers.

Now it's your turn to let your imagination run wild. Look around you – at flea markets, thrift shops, secondhand stores, your attic, your basement, and anywhere along the road. You will be amazed at the shapes that will pop out at you and just shout to you to take them home.

• Create a Family Heirloom

Another fantastic thing about mosaics is that they last and last; done properly, they will be here for generations to come. Just imagine your great-great-great grandson looking at one of your pieces and just trying to figure out what was going on in your head while you were creating. I love thinking about that, so I make my pieces to last so they will be passed down. Can you imagine the family discussing why Auntie Connie decided to create a mosaic snail for the garden? (What will be popular in the garden in the year 2500?) That snail has a much better job of being here than this book. So keep all of this in mind when choosing your projects and materials. It is good to use the best materials available to you to help ensure the longevity of your creations. You will be spending a great deal of time on some of your pieces so it makes sense to follow the instructions, use suitable adhesives, and seal the pieces when appropriate.

There were a few things that I wanted to do and just couldn't fit into my schedule. My mosaic bowling balls are conversation starters, but how about a mosaic flamingo? I am telling you, just have fun!

Just as I would tell my students, my designs are to give you a starting place. Feel your own creativity and change the design any way your imagination takes you. That is what is so much fun about mosaics – you really can't go wrong. There are very few rules in making mosaics.

Materials for Mosaics

Finished mosaics can look complicated, but mosaic techniques are simple to learn and many mosaic projects are quick and easy to do. Many mosaic materials are readily available and inexpensive, and some materials – such as broken china, seashells, and beach glass – are free or cost very little.

MATERIALS YOU WILL NEED:

• **Tesserae** – tiles, glass pieces, broken china or terra cotta – that are pieced together on a surface to create the design

• **Surfaces,** such as wood, terra cotta, cement, or metal

• **Adhesives,** such as white craft glue or a clear silicone adhesive, or indoor-outdoor mosaic glue to hold the tesserae to the surface

• **Grout,** to fill the spaces between the tesserae, smooth the surface, and add strength and durability to the mosaic. There is sanded and smooth – I use sanded 99% of the time.

• **Tools** – a few simple tools such as tile or glass nippers and a rubber mallet. ❑

Tesserae

*Tesserae are the tiles, glass pieces, broken china, or terra cotta that
are pieced together on a surface to create the design.*

CERAMIC TILES

Ceramic tiles are made from clay that has been shaped by hand or in a mold and fired. They are available in a huge array of shapes, sizes, and colors, individually and on sheets, decorated and plain, glazed and unglazed. The color of the tile may be due to the color of the clay it is made from or from a glaze that is applied before firing. Some tiles have painted designs; you can also paint or stencil your own designs on tiles with permanent enamel paints. Tiles may have a textured or smooth surface and a glossy or matte finish.

Tiles can be bought at crafts and building supply stores and specialty stores that sell tile and bathroom fixtures.

GLASS

You also can create mosaics using only pieces of glass. Some early mosaics were made only of small opaque glass cubes.

• *Stained Glass*

Stained glass pieces, cut in shapes with a **glass cutter** or broken into irregular pieces, can be used to create mosaics. Stained glass pieces are available from crafts stores and catalogs. Because stained glass is generally not as thick as tiles, you may wish to build up the surface under the glass pieces with silicone adhesive so they will be flush on the surface with thicker tiles if you use glass and tile in the same mosaic piece. Edges of unpolished glass pieces are sharp and dangerous if not grouted.

Often you can buy glass scraps by the pound from a stained glass shop for a very reasonable price. They are happy to get rid of the scraps, and you will pay lots less for smaller pieces than for large new sheets. My friend Robyn Huber has made magnificent use of colored glass and mirrors for some of the projects in this book. She favors creating mosaics with glass more than tiles.

• *Glass Tiles*

Glass tiles are small squares of patterned, colored or clear glass. They are typically sold in packages in crafts stores and stores that sell mosaic supplies.

You can also make your own glass "sandwich" tiles, using two pieces of glass and a decorative filling.

• *Mirror*

Mirror pieces can be found as small square "tiles" or in larger sizes that can be broken into irregular shapes. Various thicknesses and colors of tiles are available. You can buy mirror glass at crafts and department stores and from shops that specialize in glass and mirror. The local mirror shop that cuts mirrors for my frames was happy to save me scraps. Forget that old wives' tale about cracked mirrors bringing bad luck. I have no problem nipping and breaking mirrors into just the size I need, and my luck has only gotten better!

• *Polished Glass*

Polished glass pieces are pieces of irregular clear glass and colored textured glass that have smooth, polished edges, so they're safe to handle and use. They are typically sold in packages in crafts stores. These are great to use for ungrouted mosaics and are effective with grouting.

Molded glass shapes can be used as accents.

Continued on next page

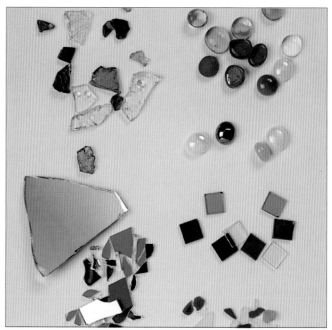

• Marbles

Flatbacked marbles are available in a wide range of clear, iridescent, metallics, and opalescent colors. They are made by melting and cooling glass pieces – when the molten glass cools on a flat surface, it assumes a rounded shape on the top while the bottom conforms to the flat surface underneath. Flatbacked marbles in various sizes are available at crafts stores and from stores and catalogs that sell supplies for stained glass.

• Beach Glass

Beach glass or "beaten glass" are pieces of glass you can find on the beach. They are likely pieces of broken bottles that have been pounded on the beach by the surf, resulting in a frosted appearance and smooth edges. You can also find commercially produced beach glass.

MIXED MEDIA

Mixed media mosaics can be made of a combination of tiles, broken china, glass, mirror, seashells, or terra cotta. I have found many of the pieces I have used in my home, my friends' homes, secondhand shops, yard and tag sales – even the trash! Soon you'll have a wonderful collection. Ask your friends and neighbors to save broken china and flower pots for your mosaics. You can reward them with a mixed media mosaic piece as a gift!

Auctions are another great source – some nights you will leave with boxes filled with goodies. Frequent attendance is the ticket to finding what you are looking for at a price you can afford. (I found myself one night bidding on a set of mah jong tiles for a piece I'd like to make, but I gave up when the price went over $100.)

• China

Broken china pieces can come from plates, bowls, cups, or saucers. Plates or saucers are the best sources because they will break into flat pieces. Store the pieces in a jar until you're ready to use them.

China nipped into shapes can be just the perfect patterned touch to your piece. I have collected so much china that I and my helpers and I are nipping it to sell. Bags of different colors and patterns, especially vintage ones, are precious to mosaicists. Think of how much fun it would be to open a bag with several hundred pieces of many colors and designs and find just the right pieces to set off the solid colors you have chosen for a design. (This of course, has given me the ideal rationale for my china addiction. I mention this in case you find yourself similarly addicted.)

• Pottery

Terra cotta pieces come from broken clay flower pots and saucers. **Broken pottery** can also create interesting looks for your designs.

• Shells

Seashells can be found at the beach for free or purchased at crafts stores. Mosaics are the solution for what to do with those leftover souvenirs of beachcombing.

• Buttons

Buttons can also be used. Everyone has a jar of old buttons – mosaics are a great place to use them. They may be

Cautions

Use care when cutting, breaking, and handling glass. Edges are sharp. Wear gloves, goggles, shoes, and protective clothing. Be sure to sweep your work area carefully to get up any stray shards, splinters, or chips. Don't let children handle glass with unpolished edges. ❏

Surfaces

Designing pieces for this book really got my imagination going. You will see how many recycled items that were used, not to mention the wonderful cement shapes that I have completely fallen in love with for both outside and inside use. You will find shapes and sizes ranging from the smallest to the tallest and the narrowest to the widest. Go with your heart, but look for pieces with surfaces that will be easy to work on. Some surfaces will be harder than others. On my Buddha Garden Statue, for instance, I decided to paint part of it gold and create a mosaic on the rest of the shape. You have that freedom when doing mosaics.

If you are just beginning, it is always good to work on a flat piece, like a stepping stone. On a stepping stone, you can transfer a design or just go free form – whatever feels most comfortable to you. Working on an item with many sides takes a bit more planning and time, as one side needs to dry before you proceed to the next side. Rounded items – such as flowerpots and bowling balls – are another challenge. I include suggestions in my instructions for these rounded shapes.

Keep your eyes open, and you will begin looking at shapes in a whole new way. When you find yourself pulling over and picking someone's trash because you spotted an interesting piece for a great mosaic, I must tell you that you most likely are becoming addicted, and you may as well start making room for your finds. In fact, if you have read this far, you are probably already addicted. Give in and have fun!

• Wood

Wood surfaces such as unfinished furniture and accessories such as frames can be purchased at crafts, department, and furniture stores. Furniture pieces such as tables and chairs and wooden accessories can be found at yard and tag sales, auctions, and thrift stores. Flat mosaic pieces also can be built on wooden planks or plywood that has been cut to any shape. You can buy wood and plywood at building supply stores.

Wood surfaces that will receive mosaics should be sealed with a clear acrylic sealer and allowed to dry before tesserae is applied.

• Ceramics & Cement

Terra cotta pots and planters are excellent surfaces for mosaics. **Cement** planters, stepping stones, and statues, decorated with mosaics, add a personal touch to your garden or patio. Find them at garden supply stores or mold them yourself. Buy the molds at crafts stores. **Glazed ceramics or china** can also be used as a base for your designs.

• Metal

Metal trays, pitchers, and bowls also are good surfaces for mosaics. Clean before using and sand to remove rust and rough spots. Look for great deals at tag and yard sales and thrift stores.

• Glass & Mirror & Plastic

You can create mosaics on trays made of glass or mirror or sturdy plexiglass. Look for sturdy pieces with smooth edges at yard sales and thrift stores. You can also have pieces of glass or mirror or plexiglass cut to shape at glass and mirror dealers. Choose material that is 1/4" thick and have them polish the edges smooth. Use stick-on felt pads on the bottom.

Other Supplies
for Creating Mosaics

Other supplies used for the projects in this book can be found at crafts stores.

Indoor/outdoor acrylic paints are used to paint trim areas of surfaces. **Acrylic craft paints** are used to tint grout. **Metallic rub-on wax** can be used to enhance molded plaster motifs, grout, and painted wood. Apply it with your always-available tool – your finger. (I find nothing works quite as well.) You can remove what's left on your finger when you're finished with nail polish remover. ❏

Pattern Drawing Supplies

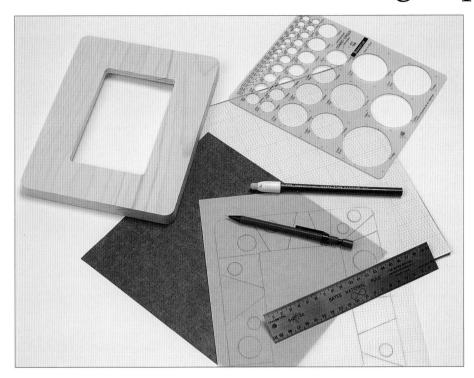

To draw your own designs, you'll want **graph paper** or brown kraft paper for making patterns, a **ruler**, a **circle template** for drawing round shapes and curves, and a **pencil**. You'll find them at crafts, arts supply, and office supply stores.

Use **transfer paper** to transfer your designs to surfaces. After transferring, outline the designs with a **permanent black marker** so the lines will be easier to see.

Protective Gear

Mosaic materials break into sharp pieces and have sharp edges. Until you become used to handling them, be especially cautious.

Protect your eyes when cutting and breaking tiles and china by wearing **protective goggles**. Wear **latex gloves** when grouting so you won't cut your fingers on any sharp edges and so the grout won't dry out your hands.

Grout

Grout is the material that fills the spaces between the tile, china, and glass pieces, adding to the strength and durability of a mosaic piece. Grouts are made of Portland cement; some grouts also contain polymers, which contribute additional strength and flexibility.

Basically, there are two kinds of grout: sanded and non-sanded. You will find you use sanded grout 99 percent of the time.

- **Non-sanded grout** is preferred for mosaics with crevices up to 1/4" wide, such as tile floors or walls, especially those made of material that is easily scratched.
- **Sanded grout** is used for everything else. Sanded grout is just that – grout with sand added to it. Use it for mosaics with larger crevices (more than 1/4").

Grout is available by the container and by the pound at crafts, hardware, tile, and building supply stores. It comes in more than 30 colors, ready to mix with water. I use buttercream most often but I love all of the colors. Some colors are more expensive than the others but when trying to get a red or grape or charcoal, don't bother trying to mix your own as it is almost impossible to get a good strong color from a light color plus a colorant.

My advice is to buy a pound of each of the really rich colors. Just the right color grout can pop the colors of a piece like nothing else will and make it a show stopper!

• Mixing Grout

When mixing your grout, use a disposable plastic container and add a wee bit of water at a time. Mix with a craft stick and just keep adding water until you get the grout to a fudge-y consistency. It should be thick enough not to drop off of your mixing stick, and you should be able to spread it like icing.

You can also mix grout in a **small plastic bucket**. If you want to use your mixing container again, clean out the leftover grout before it dries and rinse the container thoroughly. Using a disposable container is handy – you can throw it (and your leftover grout that's in it) away when you're finished. I like to use plastic yogurt containers. Wear gloves to apply grout.

Don't pour leftover grout down the sink or flush it down the toilet – it can clog your pipes. If you are sensitive to dust, **wear a mask when mixing grout.**

• Applying Grout

I like to use a little rubber spatula to apply grout, but when I teach we just use our fingers. Wear a surgical glove,

of course, because the grout will dry the heck out of your skin. There's nothing like your fingers to push the grout into every little nook and cranny.

Wipe off the excess grout with a **dry soft sponge** and allow the piece to sit for about 15 minutes. I have learned to use a dry sponge since my last book. It made sense to me that using a dry sponge was more logical. Why wet the sponge and keep rewetting the grout?

Of course, you can wipe grout the traditional way, with a wet sponge. Keep a bowl of water nearby and rinse the squeeze out the sponge often as you wipe. Wear gloves to protect your hands.

After the first 15 minutes, wipe it again. Then let it dry for another 15 minutes. Then take a soft cloth and wipe off all the tesserae until they shine. **Never** let grout dry on top of the tiles as you will find it ever so difficult to get off.

When the grout has dried, you can smooth the edges with **sandpaper**. Sandpaper can also be used to remove grout from a surface where it doesn't belong. However, you may scratch the tile surface, so it is best to remove grout before it sets.

Colorants, Adhesives & Sealers

• Colorants

White grout can be colored with **liquid or powder colorants** – you mix the colorant with the grout while you're preparing it. Mix powdered colorant with the grout powder before adding water; mix liquid colorant with the water before adding the water to the grout. Options for coloring grout include concentrated food dyes, acrylic paints, herbs, glitter, and spices. If you want a strong color, buy colored grout. Adding a colorant to white grout and getting a really strong color is nearly impossible.

You also can color the grout after it has dried on your mosaic with diluted acrylic craft paint, liquid fabric dyes (natural and otherwise), or strong coffee or tea. Experiment with the dye on pieces of dried grout to check the color before you apply it to your finished piece.

• Adhesives

A variety of adhesives can be used to glue tesserae to surfaces. The one you choose depends on the base and the mosaic materials you are using – the adhesive should be compatible with both surfaces. The adhesives used extensively in this book are white craft glue, mosaic glue and clear silicone adhesive.

White craft glue can be used for gluing flat materials (tile, flat glass, flatbacked marbles) to flat, horizontal surfaces. It holds the pieces securely, dries clear and flattens as it dries, leaving room for grout between the tile pieces

Silicone adhesive works best on curved surfaces or vertical surfaces. Because it is thick, it will hold pieces in place while drying. However, it does not flatten, so you must be careful that you don't use too much or that too much does not "ooze" between the tile pieces, leaving no room for grout. It's also the adhesive of choice when gluing for ungrouted mosaic effects and decorative glass and china pieces. Silicone adhesive also is useful when you're using materials of different thickness and you wish to build up the thinner material to be level with the others.

Mosaic Craft Glue works for both indoor and outdoor pieces and grabs quickly.

A **craft stick** is convenient spreader for glues and adhesives. *Don't* use your finger!

Mastic is a ready-to-spread adhesive sold by the bucket or the container that is applied with a trowel. Mastic is suitable for mosaics that will be used outdoors. It is generally

used on large, flat surfaces (like walls) but can be used on smaller pieces like stepping stones. Follow the manufacturer's instructions for application. Mastic is available where tile is sold.

Always read the manufacturer's instructions on glue and adhesives packages and follow all precautions and warnings. Many glues give off fumes as they dry. Avoid inhaling them and work in a well-ventilated area or outdoors.

• Sealers

It's important to seal the grout of mosaic pieces that will be used and kept outdoors.

Grout sealer is a liquid that is sold wherever grout is sold. Follow the manufacturer's recommendations for application and drying times or try this spray-on method:

1. Fill a small spray bottle halfway with grout sealer.
2. Spray the project, making sure that all of the grout is soaked.
3. Wipe the sealer off the tesserae and let dry.

Brush-on laminating liquid can be used to protect porous surfaces from the elements. Also called "pour-on resin," it is available at crafts stores.

Tools

Only a few simple, inexpensive tools are needed for creating mosaics. Many of these you may already have around your home.

• Tile Cutter

A **tile cutter** is used to score and break precise, straight cuts on flat tiles, especially ones thicker than 1/4".

• Nippers

For cutting or breaking tiles, glass, and china, you'll need **tile nippers** or **glass nippers**. They look and are handled much like pliers – some have sharp blades and others have round disks and they have spring action handles. To use them, grasp the material you want to cut or break with the nippers. When the blades or disks are pressed together, they will crack and break the material. Choose nippers that feel comfortable in your hand. *Caution: Always use goggles when nipping pieces of tile, ceramic, or glass.*

• Mallet

I use a **rubber mallet** to break plates or large numbers of tiles into irregular pieces. Some people use a *hammer,* but I don't – with a mallet, you have more control and less shattering.

• Spreaders

Use **craft sticks** or plastic spreaders to spread adhesives on the surface or to apply adhesives to individual tiles. They can also be used to fill grout into tight places or used to smooth grout on edges.

To spread grout over the glued tesserae, use a **rubber spatula** or a **plastic putty knife**.

• Tweezers

A pair of long-handled **tweezers** can be of help when you're placing small pieces.

• Brushes

A **foam brush**, **bristle paint brush**, or **artist's paint brush** can be used to paint trim and backgrounds for mosaic designs. When the grout has begun to dry, use a **stiff bristle brush** to brush away the excess.

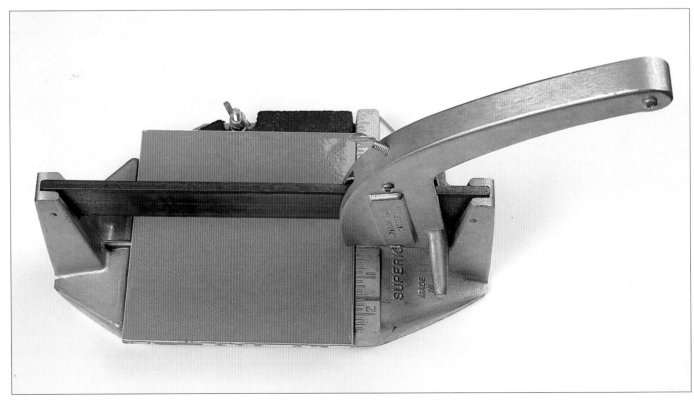

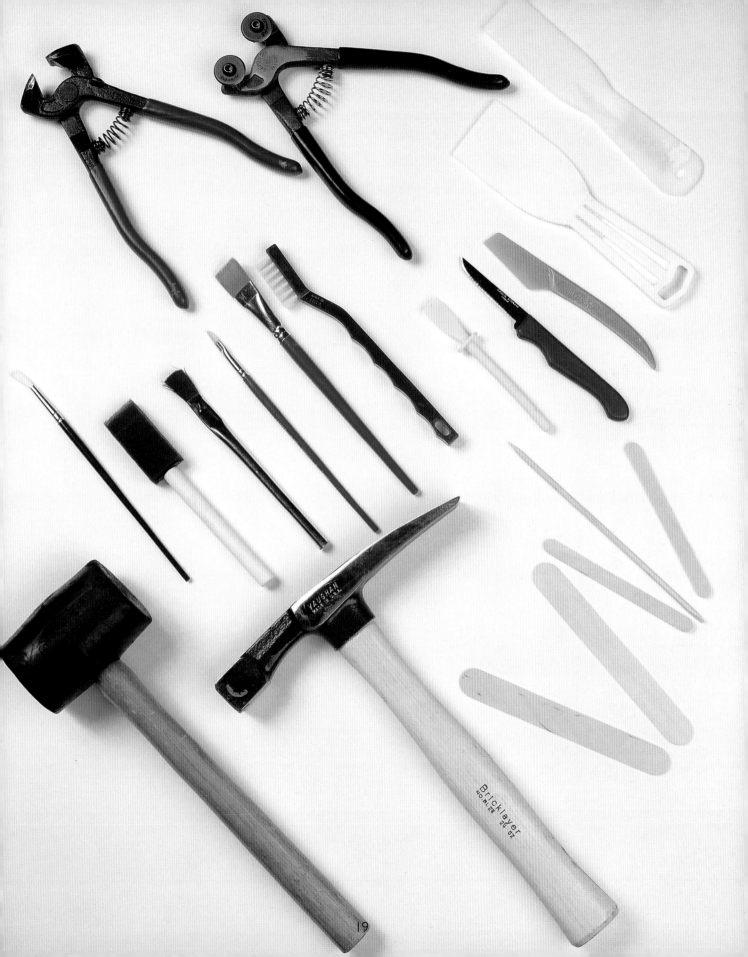

Mosaic Method

Prepare China

If you are using bits of china in your design, it is best to break it up so that you can have a variety of sizes to choose from.

1. Place the china plate between several thickness of newspaper.

2. Hold a rubber mallet at a slight angle above the plate that is between the newspaper. Hit the plate with the mallet. (**see photo 1**) *Be sure to wear safety goggles when doing this.*

3. Lift the newspaper to check the size of the pieces. The plate will break into a variety of sizes as shown (**see photo 2**). You may need to smash some more to get the sizes you need.

4. Tile Nippers can be used to cut china into specific shapes that are needed (**see photo 3**). Wear gloves and safety glasses.

Photo 2

Photo I

Photo 3

Photo 4

Prepare Tiles

5. Tiles can be found in a variety of sizes. But sometimes you will need to nip here and there on the tiles to make them fit. Using tile nippers, square tiles can be nipped into a variety of smaller shapes (**see photo 4**). Just nip about 1/8" and the tile will snap across. Tesserae do not always break perfectly – don't be concerned! That's part of the beauty and forgiving nature of mosaics. *To break a large number of tiles, china, or pottery,* place the tesserae between layers of newspaper, in a brown grocery bag, or inside a thick plastic bag. Use a rubber mallet to strike the tesserae and break them into smaller pieces.

Photo 5

Prepare Surface

6. All surfaces should be oil-free and clean. To prepare a wooden surface, sand lightly to be sure the area where the tiles will be glued is even and to smooth any part of the surface that will be painted. Wipe or brush away sanding dust.

7. Seal surfaces of wood, pottery, and cement where you're planning to glue the tesserae using clear acrylic sealer to protect them from the moisture of the grout. Let dry.

8. If needed a design can be transferred to your surface. Many of the designs in this book are free-form and don't need a pattern. But there are some patterns given for the more complicated designs. Draw or trace the design to size on graph paper or tracing paper. Then using transfer paper, transfer the design to the surface (**photo 5**).

Attach Tesserae to the Surface

9. **Spread Adhesive:** Working one small section at a time, spread glue on the project surface with a rubber spatula or a craft stick (**photo 6**). It's also a good idea to spread glue on the backs of the larger tile pieces for better contact and adhesion.

10. **Place Tiles:** Place the key design pieces (in this case, the circular tiles) first. Then position the remaining tiles, one section at a time (**photo 7**).

11. **Nip to Fit As You Go Along:** As you place the tiles, nip pieces to fit as needed (**photo 8**). This is like putting the pieces of a puzzle together. Remember they don't have to fit perfectly – that's what grout is for!

Photo 7

Photo 6

Photo 8

Photo 9

Grout the Design

12. **Mix:** Measure grout and water in a plastic container, following package instructions (**photo 9**). With experience, you'll learn to judge how much grout you need to mix.

- How much grout you need depends on the size of the piece and the space between the pieces. A larger mosaic, of course, requires more grout than a small one. A mosaic piece where the tesserae are farther apart will require more grout than a piece of the same size where the tiles are placed closer together.
- You can buy colored grout or mix in a colorant. If you're using a colorant, mix it in as you mix the grout.
- You can't save unused grout if you mix too much, so if you're not using a colorant, mix a little at a time, use that, and mix more as needed. If you're using a colorant, you need to mix all the grout you need at once so all the grout in the piece will be the same color.

13. **Spread Grout:** Using a rubber spatula, a craft stick, or your gloved fingers, spread the grout over the design and push the grout into all areas between the tiles (**photo 10**).

Photo 10

Clean Up Grout

14. **Wipe:** Fill a bowl with water. Dampen a sponge, squeezing out excess water. Wipe away excess grout. Be sure there is grout between all the tiles. If you notice a hole or empty space, fill it with grout, then wipe. Rinse the sponge, squeeze out excess water, and wipe again. Do this over and over until all the tile pieces are visible through the grout (**photo 11**). Wipe gently but thoroughly. **Option:** Use a soft dry sponge to remove excess grout. Allow to dry 15 minutes.

15. **Brush:** Before the grout is completely dry, brush away any "crumbs" of grout with a stiff bristle brush – you can use a throwaway bristle brush or old toothbrush (**photo 12**). Let dry completely.

16. **Polish:** As the grout dries, a haze or film will form over the tesserae. When the piece is completely dry, polish off the haze by rubbing with a soft cloth (**photo 13**). The tesserae will gleam.

Photo 12

Photo 11

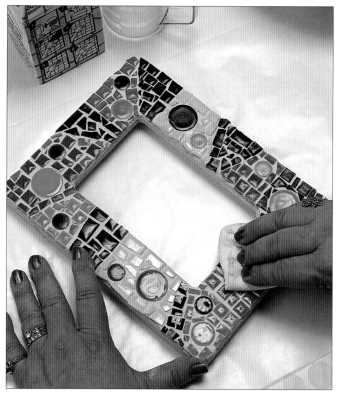

Photo 13

Photo 14

Finish the Piece

17. Sand the edges of the frame with sandpaper to smooth the edges of the grout and to remove any stray grout from the sides of the frame (**photo 14**). Wipe away dust.
18. Paint the edges of the frame with acrylic craft paint, using a foam brush or paint brush (**photo 15**). ❑

Note: You can paint your project surface before beginning the mosaic. If you do, you may need to touch up the paint after the grouting has dried. I do whatever works best for the particular project.

The grout of pieces that will be used and kept outdoors should be sealed with **grout sealer**. Follow the manufacturer's instructions.

Tips for Grouting
- Spritz the grout with water a few times during the next 48 hours. It will keep it from drying too quickly, which can cause cracking.
- If the grout should crack, mix a little of the same color grout with white glue and water to a thinner consistency than the original grout and patch the crack.

Photo 15

Mosaics with Pressed Flowers Under Glass

You can make beautiful tiles to use in your mosaics by sandwiching arrangements of pressed flowers and leaves between two pieces of glass and securing the edges with adhesive-backed foil tape. Use decorative papers, foil, or leaf to create backgrounds for the arrangements. Step-by-step instructions with how-to photos begin on page 27.

Pictured above: Terra Cotta Candle Holder

Making Glass Sandwich Tiles

Supplies

• **Glass squares**, 1/8" thick, 2 for each tile. The sizes I use most are 2" and 4" squares. In the photos that follow, 4" glass was used.

Tip: Find a glass shop in your area that is willing to cut squares of glass for you.

• **Pressed flowers, fern fronds, and leaves.** Press your own flowers or purchase packaged pressed flowers.

• **Background**, such as handmade paper, foil, or metallic leaf.

• **Adhesive**, such as a glue stick or white craft glue, to hold background paper and pressed florals in place.

• **Adhesive-backed foil tape**, to seal the edges of the glass sandwich.

• **Scissors**, for cutting the paper or trimming the flowers and leaves.

• **Tweezers**, for arranging the flowers and moving foil and metallic leaf.

• **Toothpicks**, for applying glue to flowers and leaves.

Attach Backing

Cut paper backing to size with scissors. Rub glue stick over one side of piece of glass. Press paper to glass.

Arrange Flowers

Create an arrangement with pressed flowers and greenery on the paper backing, working back to front. Hold the pressed florals with tweezers while you use a toothpick to apply tiny amounts of glue to their backs to help hold them in place.

Use the tweezers to position the pressed pieces on the paper backing.

Cover with Glass & Add Foil Tape to Edges

When your arrangement is complete, place the second piece of glass squarely on top of the first, making a sandwich. (The glass pieces are the bread, the arrangement is the filling.) Study the arrangement to be sure the result pleases you.

Wrap the edges of the glass sandwich with adhesive-backed metallic foil tape. Starting at one corner, stick the tape on and guide it all the way around the glass sandwich, making sure to smooth it as you go so as not to leave any air bubbles. Overlap the tape about 1/2" at the end. Go back and be sure it is tightly sealed – you don't want grout or moisture to leak in and spoil your sandwich tile when you grout the piece. **Caution:** Be careful – glass edges can be sharp!

TERRA COTTA CANDLE HOLDER

SUPPLIES

Terra cotta candle holder with a top
   that slants from 3" to 5"
8 tiles, 3/4" - 2 each in terra cotta,
   purple, light purple, yellow
2 pieces of 1/8" thick glass, 2" square
Adhesive-backed foil tape, 1/4" wide
Mixed color faux foil leaf
Foil leaf adhesive
Pressed pansy, ferns, leaves
Tile nippers
Tweezers
Glue stick or white glue
Sanded grout - buttercream
Toothpick
Gold metallic wax
Small scissors
Soft scrubby brush

INSTRUCTIONS

Prepare:
Nip colored tiles into pieces about 1/4"
to 1/2".

Make Glass Sandwich Tile:
1. Apply foil adhesive to one piece of the
   2" glass squares, following package
   instructions.
2. Using tweezers, place different colored pieces of foil over the adhesive.
   Allow to dry about five minutes.
3. Wipe over the foil very gently with a
   soft scrubby brush.
4. Pick up pansy with tweezers. Put a
   dot or two of white glue on the back
   of the pansy, using a toothpick.
   Position pansy on foiled background. Allow to dry.
5. Put the second piece of glass over the
   pansy. Seal the edges of the glass
   with adhesive-backed foil tape. Press
   it on well – you don't want grout or
   moisture to leak in when you grout
   the piece.

Attach Tesserae:
1. Glue glass sandwich tile to the front of the terra cotta candle.
2. Glue tile pieces all around the glass tile, mixing the colors. Let dry.

Grout:
1. Mix grout. Spread over tesserae. Wipe away excess. Let dry.
2. Wipe away haze with a soft cloth.

Finish:
Embellish the edges of the candle holder with gold metallic wax. ❑

Wonderful Mosaic Projects for Your Garden

Mosaics are especially at home outdoors, and on the pages that follow you'll find instructions for making more than 50 projects for your porch, patio, deck, garden, and backyard in these categories:

Mosaics with Localized Grouting
Mosaics without Grouting
Projects for Outdoor Living
Mosaic Stepping Stones
Outdoor Ornamental Mosaic Projects
Mosaic Pots & Planters
Mosaic Projects for Outdoor Friends

*Each project includes step-by-step instructions, a description of the surface, and a list of tesserae and other supplies for that project. For most of the projects in this book, you'll also need the **basic tools & supplies** as listed below.*

BASIC TOOLS & SUPPLIES FOR ALL PROJECTS

Tile nippers
Rubber mallet
Glue spreader or craft stick
Plastic container for mixing grout
Rubber spatula
Measuring cup
Sponge
Metal or plastic bowl

Stiff bristle brush
Soft cloth
Safety goggles
Latex gloves
For mosaics on wood surfaces:
    Wood sealer
For all projects to be kept outdoors:
    Grout sealer

Mosaics with Localized Grouting

You need not completely cover a surface with tesserae to create a mosaic. Many charming designs feature tesserae on only part of a surface, often creating a raised design. Grouting is confined to the areas with tesserae.

Pictured at right: Welcome Sign, instructions on page 34.

WELCOME SIGN

This idea came to me when I saw a wooden sign at a garden center with the word "welcome" painted on it. Immediately, I envisioned the white letters covered with multi-colored tiny tiles and grouted. I just love how it turned out – another option would be to do your family name in the same technique. What a lovely sign to have on your gate or front porch or as a housewarming gift for a special friend!

SUPPLIES

Wooden plaque, 18" x 4-1/4"
1 lb. tiles in assorted colors, 3/8"
Tile nippers
Acrylic paint - white, medium blue
1/2" paint brush
Sanded grout - white
Wood stain - dark brown
Wire and screw eyes for hanging
Adhesive of your choice
Basic tools & supplies

INSTRUCTIONS

Prepare:
1. Stain the wood. Let dry.
2. Paint the letters with white paint to use as a guide.

Attach Tesserae:
Glue tiles to cover the white letters. Nip pieces as needed to fit. Let dry.

Grout:
1. Mix grout, tinting with blue paint to make a light blue shade.
2. Spread over tiles. Carefully cut away all the extra grout with a small knife or putty knife while the grout is wet. Wipe off any excess grout from the board with a damp cloth. Let dry.
3. Wipe away haze with a soft cloth.
4. Seal grout.

Finish:
1. If the grout has stained the wood, wipe over those areas with the dark brown stain. Let dry.
2. Add wire, and you are ready to hang!

Tip:
• If you can't find a sign, make your own. Some weathered boards would be nice.

Pattern for Letters

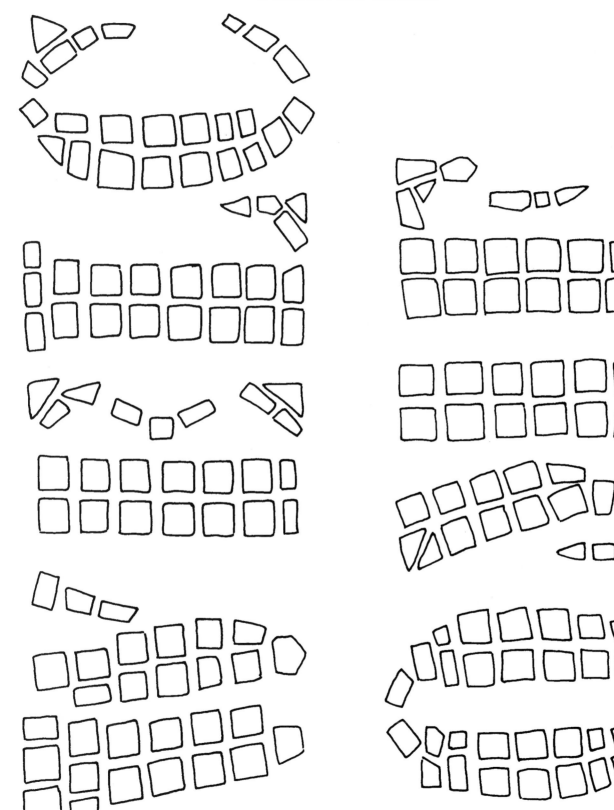

CHIMINEA

A chiminea is an outdoor terra cotta fireplace that sits on a base, or on a stand.
Chimineas come in a variety of sizes and are used for cooking or for warmth.
I just love the shape. The small and medium-sized ones also can hold a large candle
(or candles) to add flickering light to the deck or garden as the stars twinkle in
the heavens above.

SUPPLIES

Chiminea, 24" tall
Broken earthtone tiles and pottery
   or china
Faux stones with words
Stone tiles in earthtone colors
White chalk
Sanded grout - tan
Adhesive of your choice
Basic tools & supplies

INSTRUCTIONS

Prepare:
1. Draw lines on the bowl of the chiminea with chalk to mark irregularly shaped spaces to fill with tiles, broken pottery, and word stones in a freeform design. Use photo as a guide.
2. Nip pottery into pieces 1/2" to 1".

Attach Tesserae:
1. Glue the stone tiles, alternating colors, on the entire chimney of the chiminea.
2. Glue tiles, pottery, and word stones within the chalk lines. Break or nip tiles as needed. Let dry.

Grout:
1. Mix grout. Spread over tesserae. Wipe away excess. The edge of the grouting is determined by the shape of the areas with tesserae. Let dry 72 hours.
2. Wipe away haze with a soft cloth.
3. Seal the grout. ❑

Mosaics without Grouting

You also can create interesting mosaic effects without grout, using a variety of tesserae. In the ungrouted mosaic technique, the pieces are arranged on a surface and attached with clear adhesive.

GARDEN THERMOMETER

I loved this little thermometer when I saw it and decided it was just the right surface for a mosaic without grouting. The tesserae are the perfect accent just the way they are. It was quick and easy, and the results are quite charming. I am giving it to a good friend who will really appreciate it and hang it in a sheltered spot. I can always go visit it and sip cold lemonade with her on the deck.

SUPPLIES

Outdoor faux cement thermometer,
 8" tall, 3-1/2" wide
10 clear glass tiles, 1/2"
16-18 pieces of brownish yellow china
Small pieces of pressed dried flowers
Clear-drying glue
Basic tools & supplies

INSTRUCTIONS

Prepare Glass Tiles:
1. Smear a thin coat of white glue on one side of each glass tile.
2. Press a dried flower in the glue. Allow to dry.

Prepare Pottery:
Nip the pottery pieces into squares, 1/8" to 1/2".

Attach Tesserae:
1. Glue five equally spaced glass tiles on each side of the thermometer.
2. Glue pottery pieces between each glass tile.
3. Add pottery pieces to the top and bottom to finish off. ❑

Projects
for
Outdoor
Living

*When the weather cooperates, what's more
wonderful than dining and relaxing outdoors?
This section contains practical and whimsical ideas
for enhancing tables, trays, and serving pieces and
inventive accessories for decorating patios, decks,
and porches including an array of candle holders
and a decorated tabletop fountain.*

Pictured at right: White Daisies Table, instructions on page 42.

WHITE DAISIES TABLE

Pictured on page 41

Designed by Carla D'Iorio

*This table is widely available – the top is made of pressed fiberboard and is usually
shown with a table skirt. The legs screw into the bottom of the tabletop. This is
a good design for beginners. Be sure to seal the surface before you start your mosaic.
Then let the fun begin!*

SUPPLIES

Pressed fiberboard table,
   19" in diameter, 25" high
12 white tiles, 4" x 4"
2 red tiles, 4" x 4"
12 marigold yellow tiles, 4" x 4"
2 hunter green tiles, 4" x 4"
Indoor/outdoor paint - hunter green
Paint brush
Tile nippers
Sanded grout - dark green
Adhesive of your choice
Basic tools & supplies

INSTRUCTIONS

Prepare:
1. Draw design on tabletop, using photo as a guide.
2. Nip flower petal shapes from the white tiles, using the pattern provided.
3. Nip rounded flower centers from the red tiles. Don't get stressed over making them perfect.
4. Nip the marigold tiles into different sized squares (1/2" to 1-1/4"). (You can nip them down further later if you need some little fill-in pieces.)
5. Nip hunter green tiles 1/4" to 1/2" to create the stems.

Attach Tesserae:
1. Glue the red flower centers to the tabletop.
2. Glue the white petals around each center.
3. Glue the hunter green stems.
4. Glue marigold tile pieces around the outer edge of the table to make a frame.
5. Glue marigold tile pieces of various shapes to fill in around the flowers.

Grout:
1. Mix grout and apply. Wipe away excess. Let dry.
2. Wipe away haze with a soft cloth.
3. Seal the grout.

Finish:
1. Screw the legs to the table.
2. Paint the edge of the table and the legs with hunter green indoor/outdoor paint.

Tips:
• Make a round tabletop template. When you think of a design you like, sketch it out. These tables make great gifts.

• Buy a few of these tables when you see them on sale. You will always have a weekend project! ❏

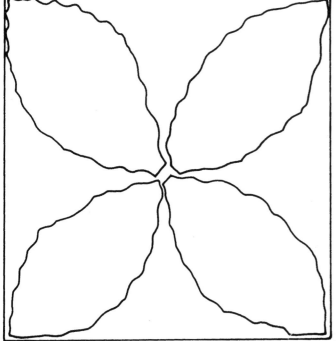

Pattern for Daisies & Leaves

Enlarge @115% for actual size.

SWIMMING FISH GAME TABLE

See instructions on page 44

SWIMMING FISH GAME TABLE

Designed by Robyn Huber

Robyn found this little outdoor table at her local grocery store. She knew she wanted to make a tile checkerboard. She started with 7/8" tiles and added little fish accents. She was so pleased with the results!

SUPPLIES

Round wooden table, 15" diameter or larger
32 deep blue tiles, 7/8"
32 white tiles, 7/8"
4 deep burgundy tiles, 7/8"
Ceramic tiles in various colors, 3/8"
Ceramic tiles, deep burgundy and lime green, 3/4"
16 glass fish shapes, various colors
24 flatbacked marbles, 12 clear and 12 deep blue (for checkers)
4 glass strips, 8" x 1/2"
Clear silicone glue
Sanded grout - white
Indoor/outdoor paint - cream
Basic tools & supplies

INSTRUCTIONS

Prepare:
1. Sand table lightly to remove any dirt and oils. Wipe off sanding dust.
2. Nip the lime green and burgundy tiles into small pieces.
3. Measure and mark the placement of the checkerboard on your table. With the border, the checkerboard measures about 10" square.

Attach Tesserae:
1. Glue the blue and white tiles to form the checkerboard.
2. Glue a deep burgundy 7/8" tile at each corner.
3. Glue the glass strips to make a border around the checkerboard.
4. Glue the 3/8" tiles around the outer edge.
5. Glue the fish shapes around the checkerboard as shown in the photo.
6. Fill in the remaining areas with lime green and deep burgundy tile pieces, placing colors as shown in photo. Let dry.

Grout:
1. Mix grout. Spread over tesserae. Wipe away excess.
2. Wipe away haze with a soft cloth.

Finish:
1. Paint the edge of the table with cream paint. Let dry 72 hours.
2. Seal the grout. ❑

EMBOSSED TILES SERVING TRAY

This is a quick and easy project. I thought a tray for taking drink and foods outside was a must for this book, and I had some very lovely tiles I found in a thrift shop that I wanted to use. This tray seemed just perfect for them.

SUPPLIES

Wooden tray with handles, 13-1/2" x 10-1/2"

5 embossed floral design tiles, 3-3/4" square

1 terra cotta floor tile, 4" square

1 beige marble-look floor tile, 4" square

14 flatbacked marbles in complementary colors

Indoor/outdoor paint - terra cotta

Sanded grout - medium blue

Adhesive of your choice

Basic tools & supplies

INSTRUCTIONS

Prepare:
Put the floor tiles between some sheets of newspaper and whack them with a rubber mallet until you have a variety of different sized pieces.

Attach Tesserae:
1. Glue the floral tiles on the tray, using the photo as a guide for placement.
2. Fill in the remaining areas with broken pieces of floor tiles, adding a few marbles here and there for interest. Allow glue to dry thoroughly.

Grout:
1. Mix grout. Spread over tesserae. Wipe away excess. Let dry.
2. Wipe away haze with a soft cloth.

Finish:
1. Sand the visible wood areas. Wipe away dust with a tack cloth.
2. Paint the tray with two coats of terra cotta indoor/outdoor paint. Let dry.
3. Seal grout.

Tips:
• Using larger tiles as the focal point of your design is great when you have only a few hours to complete a project from beginning to end.

• Watch for trays at yard sales and thrift shops. This tray was only $2 at a Goodwill store.

• You can use the same techniques with a metal tray. ❑

BLUE STARS SIDE TABLE

Designed by Robyn Huber

*Robyn bought this very inexpensive table from the school yard sale last year. One day
she started placing ceramic tiles around the edge and added some stars. Often pieces
will evolve as this one did. She added the blue glass pieces last.*

SUPPLIES

Rectangular wooden table
6 star tiles
Ceramic tiles in various deep colors
    and white, 3/8" and 7/8"
Blue glass
Clear silicone glue
Sanded grout - purple
Indoor/outdoor paint - white
Basic tools & supplies

INSTRUCTIONS

Prepare:
1. Sand table lightly to remove any dirt and oils. Wipe off sanding dust.
2. Nip the blue glass into triangular pieces.

Attach Tesserae:
1. Glue the 7/8" tiles around the edge to form the border, using photo as a guide
    for color placement.
2. Glue the star tiles.
3. Glue 3/8" tiles around the stars.
4. Glue ten 7/8" tiles around the stars, alternating colors as shown in the photo.
5. Fill in the area around the stars and inside the border with blue glass pieces. The
    glass pieces should be no more than 1/2" apart.

Grout:
1. Mix grout. Spread over tesserae. Wipe away excess. Let dry.
2. Wipe away haze with a soft cloth.

Finish:
1. Paint the edges of the table and the legs with white paint. Let dry 72 hours.
2. Seal the grout. ❏

SEA ARTIFACTS PLANT TABLE

Designed by
Connie Sheerin & Carla D'Iorio

This piece just makes me smile! The table was resurrected from a dumpster. Carla D'Iorio found it, and we collaborated on the design. Carla contributed some lovely white scallop shells. I had some little plates – one with mermaids, one with seagulls – and a great starfish pottery ashtray I found at a yard sale. The aqua plate in the center of the table is the perfect place for a plant or vase of flowers. Rather than breaking and nipping them, we used the plates whole as part of the design.

You could put it on a porch and place your favorite plant on the plate right in the middle, or, if you have a shore house, place it right inside the front door. Keep keys in the starfish and use the plates to hold other items that need a home.

Instructions follow on page 52

SEA ARTIFACTS PLANT TABLE

SUPPLIES

Table, 32" x 17", 30" tall
Various shells
Pottery or china piece with shells
   and seaweed
Mermaid plate, 3" diameter
Seagull plate, 3" diameter
4 yellow sun tiles, 2" square
5 blue shell tiles, 2" square
2 dinner plates with a fish and
   squiggle design on the rim
1 aqua plate, 8" diameter
1 yellow starfish ashtray, 5-1/2"
8 large cobalt blue flatbacked marbles
2 blue, gray, and white flecked floor
   tiles, 6" square
100 white tiles, 3/4"
18 glass fish tiles in various colors, 1"
Indoor/outdoor acrylic paint -
   royal blue
1" sponge brush
Sanded grout - white
Adhesive of your choice
Basic tools & supplies

INSTRUCTIONS

Prepare:
Make a paper template of the table shape and sketch the placement of the various elements.

Attach Tesserae:
1. Glue plates and ashtray in place.
2. Glue a border of the fish tiles and flecked floor tile pieces.
3. Fill in the space, using larger pieces first and then smaller ones.
4. Glue the 3/4" white tiles all around the edge of the table, leaving about 1/4" between each tile. Allow to dry thoroughly.

Grout:
1. Mix grout the shade of blue you prefer by adding blue paint to the white sanded grout.
2. Spread grout over the top, then the sides of the table. Wipe away excess.
3. Allow to dry, spritzing the grout with water a few times a day for the next two days as the grout dries. This helps keep the grout from cracking.
4. After 72 hours or when thoroughly dry, seal grout.

Tips:
• For a theme table like this one, it is a good idea to decide on a palette of two to three colors and then gather your materials from your stash of finds.

• Arrange the major design pieces according to your paper template before gluing. Then transfer each piece, one at a time, gluing the largest pieces first and working your way down. ❑

RETRO DINING PATIO TABLE

Ken was driving when I spotted this table that had just been put out to go to the junkyard. I certainly am grateful that Ken keeps lots of bungee cords in the back of his Jeep and doesn't ask too many questions. That is why he is my good husband!

For an abstract, fun table like this one, choose your plates first. They will be used like chargers – just place a clear plate on top for dining. Choose other pieces to complement the four plates. The wooden coasters are really quite grand and work perfectly as a place to set a glass. (You could also use square tiles of different colors.)

The word tiles that are placed around the center octopus plate add interest – and let's not forget the cat's face and the little white mouse about to run off the table.

Many thanks to Katherine Kirby, my friend and exceptional potter, for her handmade "word tiles," made in 2 Kat Studio, Wallingford, PA.

Instructions follow on page 56

RETRO DINING PATIO TABLE

SUPPLIES

White metal pedestal outdoor table,
   6' in diameter
Colorful china piece with cat's face motif
8 tiles with words
Octopus plate, 8"
White ceramic mouse, 3"
2 matching dinner plates
2 non-matching dinner plates
2-3 other broken dinner plates in
   complementary colors
1/2 lb. nipped china
4 colored wood coasters (lime, white,
   terra cotta, and blue), 4" square *or*
   4 square tiles in the same colors
130 tiles in 12 different colors, 3/4"
   (for edge of table)
Adhesive of your choice
Sanded grout - buttercream
Basic supplies & tools

INSTRUCTIONS

Prepare:
1. Nip lots of pottery and china pieces that will complement the plates you will be using whole.
2. Break the pottery piece between sheets of newspaper, using a rubber mallet.
3. Lay out all the larger pieces.

Attach Tesserae:
1. Glue the larger pieces, starting with the center and working your way out.
2. Glue the coasters in place.
3. Fill in around the center plate with a band of word tiles and pottery and then a second band of tiles.
4. Fill in the rest of the space, using clusters of colors from different plates here and there among the main pieces.
5. Glue the multi-colored 3/4" tiles around the edge of the table. Alternate the colors and leave about 1/4" between them.

Continued on next page

Grout:
1. Mix grout.
2. Spread grout over the top, then the sides of the table. Wipe away excess.
3. Allow to dry, spritzing the grout with water a few times a day for the next two days as the grout dries. This helps keep the grout from cracking.
4. After 72 hours or when thoroughly dry, seal grout.

Tips:
- Choose complementary colors to go with the main plates. I chose primary colors so anything goes!
- Because this is such a large piece of work to grout, you may have to mix several batches of grout to finish the entire piece so your grout doesn't start to dry out before you're finished. (Not to mention how tired your arms will get!) ❏

DINNERTIME CHARGER

My editor suggested I try to make a charger – she told me she had seen ones in an upscale boutique and thought they'd be easy to make. This one was made from a reject salt pottery piece I found on sale at an outlet. It was flawed in the center, but that didn't matter to me because I knew it would be covered.

Why not make a set of four or more for a gift that will withstand the test of time? They don't take long and can all be different. A charger is a good project to use up bits and pieces left from other projects. To use, place a clear glass plate on top of the mosaic charger for a gorgeous place setting.

SUPPLIES

Deep dish china plate, 11" diameter
4" round decorative tile with a favorite
    saying
18 light blue tiles, 3/4"
1 greenish blue decorative plate,
    6" diameter
10 round tiles, various sizes and colors
Miscellaneous pieces of nipped china
Acrylic craft paint - purple
Sanded grout - white
Adhesive of your choice
Clear glass plate, 9" diameter
Basic tools & supplies

INSTRUCTIONS

Prepare:
Nip the tiles, greenish blue plate, and china in pieces 1/2" to 1".

Attach Tesserae:
1. Glue round tile to the center of the deep dish plate.
2. Glue the light blue tiles to the inner edge of the plate and around the center tile.
3. Glue a row of pieces of the greenish blue plate inside the outer tile border.
4. Glue the smaller round tiles and a few flowered china pieces randomly around the large round tile.
5. Fill in the rest of the space with nipped china pieces.

Grout:
1. Mix a lavender grout using acrylic paint and white sanded grout. Apply according to general instructions.
2. Seal the grout.

Tip:
• You could also use a large terra cotta saucer as a base. ❏

Grapevines Decanter & Candlestick Holders

I bought the terra cotta wine holder and the candlesticks at a thrift shop. Somehow they seemed to belong together and needed to become a set. I can see them on a deck table, where lovers have dinner with wine by candlelight on a summer evening.

Supplies

Terra cotta wine cooler, 8-1/2" tall
2 wooden candlesticks, 5" tall
40 royal blue tiles, 3/4"
4 sq. ft. yellow stained glass
1/2 sq. ft. green stained glass
1 brown and yellow speckled china bowl
19 purplish blue iridescent round marbles
Indoor/outdoor paint - navy blue
1/2" paint brush
Sanded grout - terra cotta
Basic tools & supplies

Instructions

Prepare:
1. Sketch the placement of the grape cluster and grape leaves on the cooler.
2. Nip royal blue tiles into fourths. Make some smaller pieces.
3. Nip yellow glass into larger pieces for the cooler and smaller pieces for the candlesticks.
4. Nip green glass into medium pieces for the leaves on the cooler and smaller pieces for the candlesticks.
5. Nip pottery bowl into pieces.

Attach Tesserae:
CANDLESTICKS:
Make stripes of color, start at the top with royal blue tiles, then pottery pieces, yellow glass, green glass, yellow glass, pottery pieces, and royal blue tiles. Finish the bottom with yellow glass.

WINE COOLER:
1. Glue the marbles in place, then the leaves.
2. Trim the top edge with pieces of the speckled pottery.
3. Glue a row of the royal blue tile halves at the bottom.
4. Fill in the rest of the space with yellow glass.

Grout:
1. Mix grout. Spread over tesserae. Wipe away excess. Let dry.
2. Wipe away haze with a soft cloth.
3. Seal grout.

Finish:
Paint the bases of the candlesticks with navy blue paint. ❑

FAMILY MEMORIES SERVING CART

This was the very last piece I made for this book. I bought the serving cart at an auction. It needed some paint, but it was nice and sturdy and the tray comes off. The idea for it came a few days after my daughter's surprise birthday party. To decorate her cake, I gathered a collection of pictures of her through the years, had color copies made, and stuck them on different heights of skewers all over a sheet cake. Everyone loved the pictures. I decided to do something permanent with those pictures, and making picture tiles came to me when I was looking at this cart. What a wonderful memory piece for my mother and a family heirloom for sure!

SUPPLIES

Serving cart with removable tray,
   16" X 26" with clear glass center
155 light pink tiles, 3/4"
4 pieces of clear glass, 1/8" thick,
   4" square
16 pieces clear glass, 1/8" thick,
   2" square
4 floral motif tiles, 4-3/8" square
2 raised motif floral tiles,
   3-3/4" square
1 white tile, 4-1/8" square with a
   2-1/4" square opening

A variety of pressed dried flowers
Copper or silver self-adhesive foil tape,
   1/4" wide
Indoor/outdoor paint - metallic gold
Medium paint brush
Variety of color-copied photographs
Decorative textured papers
White glue
Deckle edge scissors
Tweezers
Sanded grout - mauve
Basic tools & supplies

INSTRUCTIONS

Prepare:
1. Gather color copies of a group of pictures you want to use. on your piece.
2. Make a paper template of your design.

Make Glass Tiles:
1. Choose the pictures and cut them with deckle edge scissors to fit two 4" and five 2" squares. If the pictures are smaller than the glass, add a decorative paper background so the tile will be opaque. Glue the paper to the bottom piece of glass with white glue. Embellish with tiny bits of dried flowers and add the photocopied photo.
2. Top with a piece of glass and wrap edges with foil tape. See the Basic Techniques section for how-to photos and detailed instructions.

Attach Tesserae:
1. Glue the picture tiles and floral motif tiles in place. Start in the corners and work toward the center.
2. Fill in with 3/4" pink tiles. You may have to nip some of them to fit. Allow to dry thoroughly.

Grout:

1. Mix the grout. Spread up to but not over the glass tiles (you don't want to scratch the glass) and over the other tesserae. Wipe away excess. Let dry.

2. Polish the haze with a soft cloth.

3. Seal the grout. Let dry.

Finish:

1. Paint the wooden trim of the tray with gold metallic paint.

2. Paint the rest of the cart with gold or pink or a combination of the two – your choice. ❑

COLORED GLASS VOTIVE HOLDERS

Designed by Robyn Huber

"Votives are fun and quick and so easy that kids can make them," says Robyn. "And the votives can be used right away!"

For the sun votive, Robyn used little tiny pieces of glass in red, yellow, and orange radiating out from the center, filled in the space with black glass, and finished it off with black grout. The blue star votive used star-shaped glass accent pieces and irregularly shaped blue triangles.

"Connie gave me a jelly jar," says Robyn, and the tall glass votive idea was the result. "The top was not smooth since the jar had a twist-off lid. I glued glass flowers around the top and along the sides, where I also used glass strips and glass tiles."

Sun & Moon Votives

SUPPLIES

Clear glass votive
Clear silicone glue
Stained Glass pieces
Sanded grout (preferably a dark color)
Cloth rag, such as an old hand towel
Basic tools & supplies

INSTRUCTIONS

Prepare:
1. Select the glass you want to use. Choose at least some glass that will let the fire show.
2. Cut glass shapes. The pieces should not be any bigger than 3/4" on a side.

Attach Tesserae:
Use a cloth rag to lay your votive on so it won't roll around while you work. Using a craft stick, apply glue to each piece of glass and place it on the votive. Place pieces no more than 1/2" apart. (They can be as close as you like.) Be careful not to apply too much adhesive. If the adhesive gets on the top side of the glass it must be wiped off immediately. Glue all the glass on one side before moving to another side.

Grout:
1. Mix the grout. Spread over the tesserae. Remove excess. Keep turning the votive to make sure you have grouted all sides.
2. Using a small brush, brush off any remaining grout. With a damp paper towel or cloth, wipe off the glass. Let dry 72 hours.
3. Wipe away haze with a soft cloth.
4. Seal the grout.

Tip:
• You only have to seal the grout on your votive if you are planning to leave it outside for extended periods. ❏

Tall Glass Votive Holder

SUPPLIES

Glass jelly jar
Stained Glass pieces in a variety
    of shapes and colors
12 glass flowers
Sanded grout - purple
Clear silicone glue
Basic tools & supplies

INSTRUCTIONS

Prepare:
Cut glass into strips, squares, and rectangles.

Attach Tesserae:
1. Glue flower shapes around top of jar, placing them so they stand up above the edge of the jar.
2. Glue remaining flower shapes on sides of the jar.
3. Glue vertical strips and rows of rectangles on sides of jar around glass flowers. Let dry.

Grout:
1. Mix the grout. Spread over the tesserae. Remove excess. Keep turning the votive to make sure you have grouted all sides.
2. Using a small brush, brush off any remaining grout. With a damp paper towel or cloth, wipe off the glass. Let dry 72 hours.
3. Wipe away haze with a soft cloth.
4. Seal the grout if you plan to keep it out in the weather. ❑

ON THE BEACH SUMMERTIME FRAME

Designed by Carla D'Iorio

This frame isn't something you would use in the backyard, but it would be fine to use on a screened porch. It brings the outdoors inside, and it's a great way to use those shells we all collect on the beach. Every time you look at it, you can remember the warmth of the sun and the sound of the waves.

SUPPLIES

Wooden frame, 7" x 9" with 4" x 6" opening

1 lb. assorted tiles, 3/8" (for the sky)

Pieces of tile or china in blue and brown (for the water and the boat)

Round tiles - 1 yellow (for the sun), 7 white, light gray, or light blue (for the sail and clouds)

Shells from the beach

Acrylic craft paint - navy blue

1/2" paint brush

Sanded grout - white

Adhesive of your choice

Basic tools & supplies

INSTRUCTIONS

Prepare:
1. Sketch a design on the frame using photo as a guide.
2. Pick out all the shades of blues, from light to dark in the 3/8" tiles.
3. Nip some smaller pieces of darker blue tiles or china to form the water line above the beach.
4. Nip some pieces of shell for the beach, leaving some whole shells for accent.
5. Nip the round tiles for the sail and clouds in half. Select other shapes and nip pieces as needed.

Attach Tesserae:
1. Glue the sun, clouds, boat, and clouds to the frame.
2. Glue the blue tiles, starting from the top down to the beach line.
3. Glue pieces of shells and whole shells on the beach area of the frame.

Grout:
1. Mix grout. Spread over tesserae. Wipe away excess. Let dry.
2. Wipe away haze with a soft cloth.

Tip:
• When you clean the grout off the shells, use an old toothbrush to get grout out of the crevices. (Of course, this is the beach, and sand does get in the shells!) ❏

GLISTEN & TRICKLE TABLETOP FOUNTAIN

I found this fountain in a chain store. I loved the idea that it had a raised design and the moment I saw it, I decided to use iridescent materials that would look like water. The effect is fabulous and soothing. Use it as a Feng Shui water feature to give your deck just the right energy! Make one and then sit, meditate, and relax!

SUPPLIES

Cast stone flower fountain, 11-3/4" wide, 7-1/2" deep, 15-3/4" tall
84 tiles in green, blue, and lavender hues, 3/8"
20 blue iridescent flatbacked marbles
20 peridot green mirror tiles, 1/2"
20 cobalt blue mirror tiles, 1/2"
50 pieces of irregularly shaped mirror
Sanded grout - medium blue
Adhesive of your choice
Basic tools & supplies

INSTRUCTIONS

Prepare Mirror:
Nip silver mirror pieces to fit around the flower.

Attach Tesserae:
Remember to leave space at the bottom of the piece where it sits in the base.
1. Glue the 3/8" tiles in two rows on either side, alternating the colors.
2. Glue a few marbles and colored mirror pieces here and there on either side of the flower.
3. Fill in the area with irregular pieces of mirror.
4. Glue some colored mirrors and marbles on the base.

Grout:
1. Mix grout. Spread over tesserae up to but not over the flower. Wipe away excess. Carefully wipe any grout from the flower. Let dry.
2. Wipe away the haze with a soft cloth. ❏

See closeup view on page 70

Pictured above: A closeup view of Glisten & Trickle Tabletop Fountain. 70

MINI ADIRONDACK CHAIR

When my eye caught this little wooden chair in the local wicker outlet store I was thrilled. It reminded me of the wooden chairs we had sitting in our backyard when I was a little girl. Summer evenings seemed to last forever. As twilight came, we all sat in the backyard sipping Mom's homemade iced tea, watching my little brother and sister catching fireflies in jelly jars with holes in the lids. It was peaceful – and there was time in the day to enjoy each other and the beauty of nature.

To make the checkerboard mosaic, I picked out the light and dark aqua tiles out of a pound of 3/8" tiles and had plenty left over. The chair came painted a very dark green, which I embellished with patina wax from a craft store. When I realized how easy it was and how great it looked when I finished, I wished I had gotten a set of four!

SUPPLIES

Wooden adirondack chair,
   9-1/2" high, 6" deep, 8" wide
Patina wax
39 light aqua tiles, 3/8"
39 dark aqua tiles, 3/8"
Sanded grout - blue-green
Adhesive of your choice
Basic tools & supplies

INSTRUCTIONS

Attach Tesserae:
Glue the tiles in a checkerboard pattern on the chair arms and apron, using the photo as a guide.

Grout:
1. Mix grout. Spread over tiles one section at a time. Wipe away excess. Let dry.
2. Wipe away haze with a soft cloth.

Finish:
Using your finger, rub wax lightly over the slats of the chair – not too much, not too little, but just right! Practice using the wax on the underside of the chair (where it won't show).

Tip:
• When you see a piece like this little Adirondack chair, take home a bag full and make extras to give as gifts. ❏

Mosaic Stepping Stones

Stepping stones are useful (they keep your shoes and feet clean and dry), beautiful (they add color and interest all year long), and — best of all — they are easy and quick to make. Use them in sets or as accents.

You can buy stepping stones in a variety of sizes and shapes at home improvement stores and garden centers. At crafts stores, you can buy molds and mediums for molding your own stepping stones.

Pictured at right: Bright Flowers Stepping Stone, instructions on page 74.

BRIGHT FLOWERS

Pictured on page 73

At a chain plant store in our area I came across some really ugly stepping stones. Apparently they were very old stock (only three were left in the store), and the price was very low. I am sure not even the manager thought anyone would buy them, but, of course, I did! I wish you could have seen the cashier's face when she asked me if I was sure I wanted all three. I am still chuckling! You just never know where you will find a good surface!

SUPPLIES

Stepping stone, 12"
2 lbs. leaf-shaped tiles in assorted sizes and colors
1/2 lb. round tiles in assorted sizes and colors
100 white tiles, 3/4", or white china pieces
Indoor/outdoor paint - dark blue
1" paint brush
Sanded grout - pewter
Adhesive of your choice
Basic tools & supplies

INSTRUCTIONS

Prepare:
1. Make a paper template of the stepping stone and lay out how many flowers you want and where you want them placed. You will need five leaf tiles for the petals for each flower and one circle for each flower center.
2. Nip lots of white tiles so once your flowers are glued down you will be able to begin filling in the background.

Attach Tesserae:
1. Glue flowers according to your paper template.
2. Glue white tile pieces to fill in around flowers. Make sure you use flat pieces along the outside edges. This frames your piece and helps keep the grout from falling off the edges.

Grout:
1. Mix grout. Spread over tiles. Wipe away excess. Let dry.
2. Wipe away haze with a soft cloth.
3. Seal the grout.

Finish:
Paint the outer edge with dark blue paint. Let dry. ❑

Patterns for Flowers

Enlarge @ 170% for actual size.

74

FLOWERS AND HUMMINGBIRD

Designed by Robyn Huber

Robyn made this stepping stone using pre-cut glass pieces for the bird and flowers. When the border, flowers, and bird were in place, she filled in the space with complementary colors. This is a great project for a beginner.

SUPPLIES

Stepping stone, irregular round shape, 12" diameter
Pre-cut glass shapes - 4 tulips in various colors, 1 hummingbird
Dark green stained glass
Light blue marbled stained glass
Dark blue stained glass
Pink stained glass
Clear silicone glue
Sanded grout - purple
Basic tools & supplies

INSTRUCTIONS

Prepare:
1. Cut irregular strips of green and light blue marbled glass.
2. Cut 3/4" squares of dark green and dark blue glass.
3. Cut rectangles about 1/4" x 3/4" from light blue marbled glass.
4. Cut irregular triangles from pink and remaining light blue marbled glass.

Attach Tesserae:
Glue the glass in this order: border of dark green and dark blue glass squares alternating with light blue marbled rectangles, strips for tulip stems and leaves, tulip flowers, hummingbird, filler pieces. Apply adhesive to the back of each piece with a craft stick and glue glass to the stepping stone. Place pieces no more than 1/2" apart. (They can be as close as you want.) Be careful not to apply too much adhesive. If the adhesive gets on

the top side of the glass, wipe it off immediately.

Grout:
1. Mix grout. Apply to tesserae. Removing any excess grout as you go along. Using a small brush, brush off any remaining grout. Let dry.
2. Wipe away haze with a soft cloth.
3. After 72 hours, seal the grout. ❑

75

EMBOSSED IRIS

I spotted this stepping stone with a raised design in a garden store and knew it was just the thing to go with my tabletop fountain. I decided to do a watercolor effect of color around the flowers. After it was grouted with buttercream grout, I felt it needed something so I used the multi-color grout technique.

SUPPLIES

Stepping stone with raised floral design, 12" diameter
2 floral patterned china dinner plates
Stained glass pieces - greens, pinks, and blues
Glass paint - yellow
Indoor/outdoor acrylic paint - green, pink, blue
Cosmetic sponge wedges
Sanded grout - buttercream
Adhesive of your choice
Basic tools & supplies

Creating Multi-Colored Grout

The multi-colored grout adds interest to your piece and is a great technique to use when you want to change the grout color. Allow grout to dry for at least 30 minutes before dyeing. Of course, it's fine if the grout is entirely dry. This must be done **before** the grout is sealed. *Here's how:*

1. Mix a squirt of acrylic paint with water to make several color washes that complement the colors of your design. Mix each in a separate container.
2. Sponge on colors, one at a time onto your finished piece, staining and coloring the grout. Sponge large areas of one color then change to another color so that it looks like one color fades into the next. Wipe color from the tiles. Let dry completely (overnight). ❑

INSTRUCTIONS

Prepare:
1. With a pencil, draw guidelines where you want the colors to begin and end.
2. Nip the edges of the dinner plates to make pieces for the border.

Attach Tesserae:
1. Glue the pieces from the edges of the dinner plates around the edges of the stepping stone.
2. Glue the green, pink, and blue glass pieces around the iris in the three marked-off areas. Shade and mix the different tones of each color family.

Grout:
1. Mix grout. Apply to tesserae. Wipe off excess. Use a toothbrush to remove grout from the raised flower design. Let dry.
2. Wipe away haze with a soft cloth.
3. Dilute acrylic paint colors with water and sponge the green on the green area, the pink on the pink area, and the blue on the blue area of the design. See instructions in the box. Let dry.
4. Seal grout.

Finish:
Paint flower centers with yellow glass paint.

SERENITY STEPPING STONE & GARDEN BUDDHA

This stepping stone with the Asian flair and the Buddha statue are a perfect pair for the garden. They're photographed with some little brass hanging lights I bought as an accent piece. I glued a few colored marbles to them to tie it all together. I could also envision these pieces around a fish pond. Serenity!

Stepping Stone

Ah! Sometimes you just get lucky and find a really unusual surface like this stepping stone. The pattern was there and ready for me – all I had to do was to decide what colors to use. It looked Asian to me, so I decided to go with the red and black tiles and red and black grout. The gold enamel paint seemed to be the perfect embellishment.

SUPPLIES

Stepping stone with cut out and raised design, 11" square
100 red tiles, 3/4"
15 black tiles, 3/4"
Enamel paint - metallic gold
Small paintbrush
Sanded grout - black, red
Adhesive
Basic tools & supplies

INSTRUCTIONS

Prepare:
1. Nip the red tiles in quarters. You will have to nip some smaller pieces to fill in.
2. Nip the black tiles in thirds and nip the thirds in half again. You will need to nip some smaller pieces to fill in.

Attach Tesserae:
1. Glue the red tiles.
2. Glue the black tiles.

Grout:
1. Mix black grout and apply.
2. Mix and apply the red grout. Allow to dry thoroughly.
3. Seal. Let dry.

Finish:
Apply gold metallic paint to the raised part of the design. ❑

Garden Buddha

I just could not resist this wonderful little Buddha – I immediately saw him with a coat made of Japanese or Chinese patterned china. I found six small saucers at a yard sale for a few dollars and used them to create his jacket. The color on the edges of the plates became the trim on his robe.

SUPPLIES

Cement Buddha, 9-1/4" tall, 7" wide at the base
6 china plates with Oriental design

Enamel paint - metallic gold
Medium paint brush
Sanded grout - buttercream

Clear silicone adhesive
Basic tools & supplies

INSTRUCTIONS

Prepare:
1. Nip china into many small and different sized pieces (1/2" and smaller).
2. Nip the rims of the plates into small pieces for trim of his robe.

Attach Tesserae:
1. Glue the trim of the robe.
2. Fill in the rest of the coat with nipped pieces of china.

Grout:
1. Mix grout. Spread over tesserae. Wipe away excess. Let dry.
2. Wipe away haze with a soft cloth.
3. Seal grout. Let dry.

Finish:
Paint the rest of the Buddha with gold paint. Let dry.

Tip:
• If you have a lazy Susan or turntable, you will find dressing the Buddha with tiles much easier! The cement statue is a bit heavy to keep turning by hand. ❑

MIRRORS AT YOUR FEET

Designed by Robyn Huber

"I was at my sister Melannie's house helping her with a mosaic bird bath," says Robyn. "She had these square stepping stones. I started working with square and rectangular glass pieces, creating pairs and gluing them to opposite corners. It created itself as I cut the pieces."

SUPPLIES

Stepping stone, 11" square
Stained glass in various deep colors
Mirror glass
Clear silicone glue
Sanded grout - purple
Basic tools & supplies

INSTRUCTIONS

Prepare:
Using the pattern provided, cut glass shapes.

Attach Tesserae:
Apply adhesive to the back of each piece with a craft stick and glue glass to the stepping stone. Place pieces no more than 1/2" inch apart. (They can be as close as you want.) Be careful not to apply too much adhesive. If the adhesive gets on the top side of the glass, wipe it off immediately.

Grout:
1. Mix grout. Apply to tesserae. Removing any excess grout as you go along. Using a small brush, brush off any remaining grout. Let dry.
2. Wipe away haze with a soft cloth.
3. After 72 hours, seal the grout. ❑

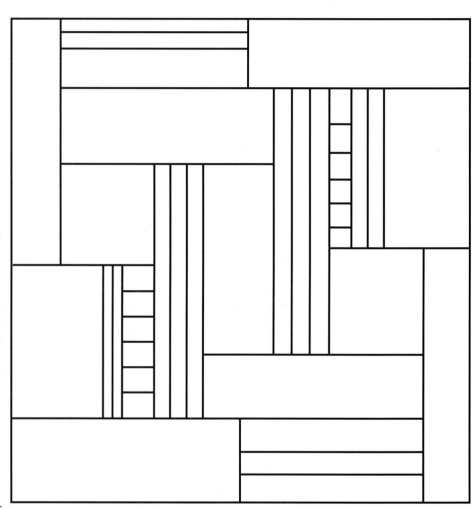

Enlarge pattern @220% for actual size.

FROG CROSSING

This stepping stone came about one night when I was shopping online – the frog motif seemed absolutely perfect for an outdoor stepping stone. I kept bidding on that group of china, determined to get it. I just love the friendly look on froggie's face – I look at it and smile. This is one of those things I write about in my gratitude journal!

SUPPLIES

Octagonal stepping stone, 12"
Frog motif china piece or tile, 4"
Pieces of china with frog motifs from
    several plates
4 jade green flatbacked marbles, 2"
15 luster green flatbacked marbles, 1"
4 luster pink flatbacked marbles, 1"
10 luster white flatbacked marbles, 1"
8 acrylic glow-in-the-dark flatbacked
    stones
Sanded grout - white
Acrylic craft paint - neon green
Indoor/outdoor paint - green
1" brush
Adhesive of your choice
Basic tools & supplies

INSTRUCTIONS

Attach Tesserae:
1. Glue 4" frog motif piece at center.
2. Glue the smaller froggies.
3. Glue pink flowers. They are made with luster pink flatbacked marble centers and nipped china pieces for petals.
4. Glue jade flatbacked marbles and acrylic pieces.
5. Ring the center piece with white marbles.
6. Glue the green marbles and tiles around the outer edge.
7. Fill in the open spaces with the other pieces of china.

Grout:
1. Mix white grout and tint with neon green acrylic paint.
2. Spread over tiles. Wipe away excess. Let dry.
3. Wipe away haze with a soft cloth.
4. Seal grout.

Finish:
Paint the edges with green indoor/outdoor paint. Let dry.

Tips:
• I lucked out and found these china pieces pre-cut. To prepare them yourself, find a few dinner plates with a theme, cut the center motif in a 4" circle using your china nippers, and nip the rest into pieces.

• Be on the lookout for plates with a theme. You will be surprised what you can find in discount stores and chain stores that sell sets of dishes in a box! ❏

83

IVY STRIPES

Designed by Robyn Huber

Robin's seven-year-old daughter Kelsea brought home a drawing that she created of alternating pink and green sections. She told Robyn they should make it into a stepping stone, and so they did! Robyn cut the big pieces and Kelsea worked with the smaller pieces. Kelsea is quite proud of her stepping stone. I am sure it will become a family heirloom.

SUPPLIES

Stepping stone, 11" square
Green pebbled stained glass
Pink and white marbled stained glass
Stained glass pieces in a variety of
    deep greens and blues
Clear silicone glue
Sanded grout - pink
Basic tools & supplies

INSTRUCTIONS:

Prepare:
1. Cut three green glass strips, 1-1/2" x 8-3/4".
2. Cut four pink marbled glass strips, 1-1/2" x 8-3/4".
3. Cut three pink marbled glass pieces, 2-1/8" x 1-1/2"
4. Cut deep green and blue glass into a variety if triangular pieces.

Attach Tesserae:
Apply adhesive to the back of each piece with a craft stick and glue glass to the stepping stone, using photo as guide for placement. Place pieces about 1/4" apart. Be careful not to apply too much adhesive. If the adhesive gets on the top side of the glass, wipe it off immediately.

Grout:
1. Mix grout. Apply to tesserae. Removing excess grout as you go along. Using a small brush, brush off any remaining grout. Let dry.
2. Wipe away haze with a soft cloth.
3. After 72 hours, seal the grout. ❑

Outdoor Ornamental Mosaic Projects

Mosaics are a great way to embellish and decorate garden ornaments and statues, adding color and design. A mosaic gazing ball – made on a discarded bowling ball – is a sure-fire conversation starter. If you put your creation in the front yard, it's sure to invite comments. The fun part is when they ask you what it is made from!

Pictured at right: Dragonfly Jewel Garden Ornament or Stepping Stone, instructions on page 88.

DRAGONFLY JEWEL
GARDEN ORNAMENT

Pictured on page 87

*When I found this Stepping Stone in a garden center it looked like a dragonfly but
with the mosaics, it reminds me more of a butterfly. Call it what you like – you
will be transfixed when you see how it glitters in the sun. You are just going to
love how the mirror pieces reflect the glorious colors in your garden and the sky.
Because of the fragility of the tiles, I use this piece placed among my flowers
rather than as a stepping stone.
This is a great beginners' piece – it can be made in an afternoon.*

SUPPLIES

Dragonfly cement stepping stone,
    13-1/4" wing span, 9-1/2" long
Textured glass plate, 8" diameter
1 china dinner plate with floral design
100 silver embossed mirror tiles, 1/2"
12 metallic lime green glass tiles, 1"
2 bright pink flatbacked Austrian
    crystals
Enamel spray paint - gold metallic
Adhesive of your choice
Sanded grout - pewter
Basic tools & supplies

*A pattern is provided for the butterfly
shape. It can be used to cut a wood
shape to use for a hanging garden
ornament.*

INSTRUCTIONS

Prepare:
1. Spray the back of the textured glass plate with two to three coats of gold metallic
    spray paint, allowing each coating to dry thoroughly.
2. Nip the sprayed glass pieces into pieces 1/2" to 1".
3. Nip floral patterned china into pieces 1/2" to 1".
4. Nip each metallic lime green glass tile into four pieces.

Attach Tesserae:
1. Start with the body, gluing the metallic green pieces to cover about halfway.
2. Glue gold-sprayed glass pieces on the rest of the body in rows.
3. Glue the gold-sprayed glass pieces on the tips of the wings.
4. Fill in the wings, starting with a china row and then a mirror row. On the second
    wing, start with another row of the embossed mirror tiles.

Grout:
1. Mix grout. Spread over tesserae. Remove excess. (The pewter grout really shows
    off the mirrors.) Let dry.
2. Wipe away haze with a soft cloth.
3. Seal grout. ❑

Pattern for
Butterfly Shape

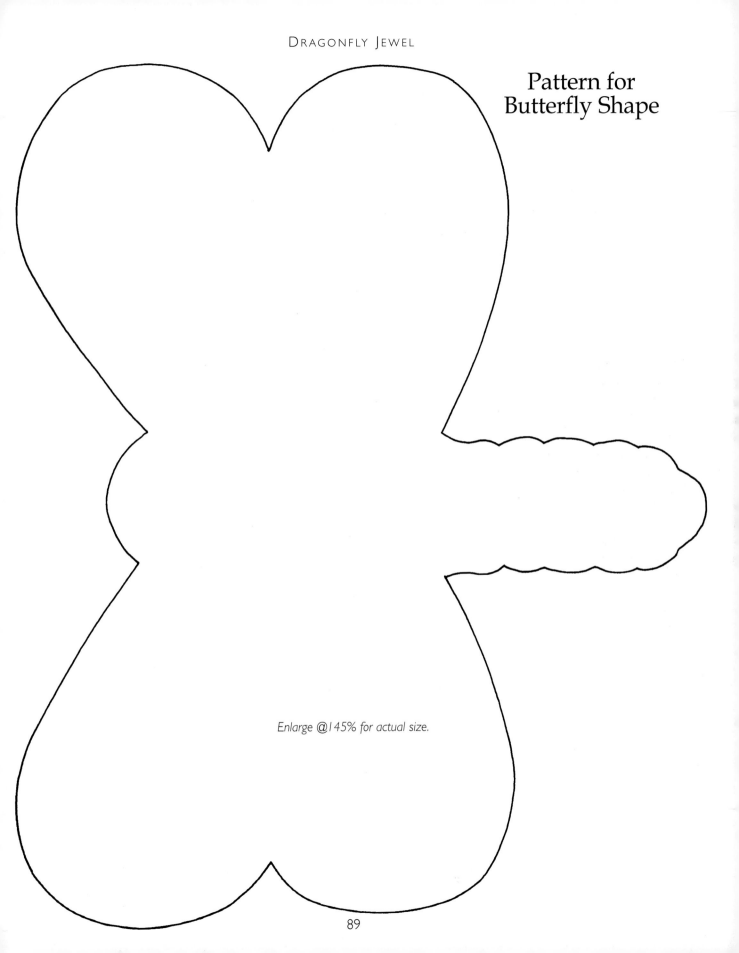

Enlarge @145% for actual size.

GARDEN CHAIR

Designed by Carla D'Iorio & Connie Sheerin

*Carla loves to pick trash as much as I do and may be even better at it than I am.
We envisioned this old ladderback chair with no seat as the perfect thing to hold a
plant or a basket of fresh picked vegetables and Angel, my dog.
We left the rest of the chair its natural color to add more contrast and interest.*

SUPPLIES

Wooden ladderback chair
3 iridescent Japanese china plates with
   floral and bird designs
8 glass flowers (red, cobalt blue,
   yellow), 1"
12 red tiles, 3/4"
12 orange tiles, 3/4"
Piece of chicken wire slightly larger
   than the missing chair seat
Staple gun
Sanded grout - medium blue
Adhesive of your choice
Basic tools & supplies

INSTRUCTIONS

Prepare:
1. Nip the china plates in large pieces. Leave the edges intact.
2. Nip the orange and red tiles into small pieces.
3. Place chicken wire over chair rungs. Staple in place. Allow some slack for the basket or planter to sit in.

Attach Tesserae:
1. Arrange pieces of the china plates on each piece of the back of the chair.
2. Fill in the open spots with pieces of red and orange tiles.

Grout:
1. Mix grout. Spread over tesserae. Wipe away excess. Let dry.
2. Wipe away haze with a soft cloth.
3. Seal grout.

Finish:
Glue glass flowers here and there for embellishment.

Tip:
• Fill in the space around the basket on the chicken wire with Spanish moss. ❑

HEARTS & FLOWERS GAZING BALL

This gazing ball idea happened a few years ago when I was asked to do something creative with an old bowling ball. Having been a disco dancing queen in my day, I immediately thought of combining the disco ball and gazing ball looks to create a conversation piece for the garden.
Victorians used gazing balls in their gardens to check who was approaching from behind or the side so as not to be shocked. They were also used by Victorian chaperons to keep an eye on courting couples.

SUPPLIES

Used bowling ball
Plastic or wood putty
1 lb. assorted flatbacked marbles - cat's eyes, opaque, clear, frosted, iridescent
1 lb. assorted color square tiles, 3/8"
1/2 lb. assorted china pieces
1 lb. assorted pastel ceraminc tile shapes - ovals, hexagons, rectangles
1 lb. heart-shaped tiles in assorted colors, 1"
Mirror tiles, 1/2"
1 lb. tiles in assorted shapes
Acrylic craft paints in vibrant colors - purple, neon green, yellow, deep pink, bright yellow, turquoise, orange
Cosmetic sponges
Sanded grout - buttercream or white
Old towel
Clear silicone adhesive
Basic tools & supplies

INSTRUCTIONS

Prepare:

1. Clean bowling ball well with soap and water. Fill the holes with plastic or wood putty. Allow a couple of days for the putty to dry thoroughly since the finger holes are fairly deep.
2. Nip some of the larger tiles into pieces so they will lie on the rounded surface.
3. Nip the china pieces to size.

Creating Multi-Color Grout

*Allow grout to dry for at least 30 minutes before dyeing. Of course, it's fine if the grout is entirely dry. This must be done **before** the grout is sealed. Here's how:*

1. Mix a squirt of acrylic paint with water to make several color washes that complement the colors of your design. Mix each in a different container.
2. Sponge colors on sections of the ball, dying and coloring the grout. Overlap colors that go well together when blended so some of the color bleeds into the color next to it. Wipe paint from tiles. Let dry completely (overnight). ❑

---

4. Lay out lots of little groups of designs that you may want to incorporate all over the ball. This will make your ball very interesting to view at any angle.

Attach Tesserae:

1. Set your ball on a bunched up towel to keep it from rolling as you work. Group colors and glue tiles and china pieces in sections. Let each section dry thoroughly before going onto the next one.
2. After you finish all of the sections, go back over it and fill in with bits and pieces so all the colors work together. Let dry.

Grout:

1. Mix grout. Spread over tesserae. Wipe off excess. Let dry.
2. Wipe away haze with a soft cloth.
3. Color grout, using the multi-color technique. See "Creating Multi-Color Grout."
4. Seal with grout sealer.

Tips:

• Call your local bowling alley and ask for "damaged" and "worn-out" balls. They will be happy to recycle them to you. Although I have always offered, no one has ever asked me or my students to pay for one. (But who knows what will happen if there is a huge demand for used bowling balls!)
• This is a good place to use up bits and pieces left from other projects.
• Look for a great gazing ball stand to show off your work of art. ❑

GLASS TRIANGLES GAZING BALL

Designed by Robyn Huber

Says Robin, "Simple designs can create a beautiful piece, and I love triangles. They fit together on anything. You may want to start with simple cuts such as triangle or squares for your first attempt. The ball looks wonderful in my garden."

SUPPLIES

Used bowling ball
Stained glass pieces, various colors and mirror
Plastic or wood putty
Clear silicone glue
Sanded grout - purple
Old towel
Basic tools & supplies

INSTRUCTIONS

Prepare:
1. Clean bowling ball well with soap and water. Fill the holes either with plastic or wood putty. Allow a couple of days for the putty to dry thoroughly.
2. Cut glass in triangles. (They do not have to be perfect!) The pieces should not be any bigger than 1-1/2" on a side.

Attach Tesserae:
Set your ball on a bunched up towel to keep it from rolling as you work. Glue glass triangles to ball in sections, using clear silicone glue. Place pieces no more than 1/2" apart. Be careful not to apply too much adhesive. If the adhesive gets on the top side of the glass, wipe it off immediately. Let each section dry thoroughly before going onto the next one.

Grout:
1. Mix grout. Spread over tesserae. Wipe off excess. Let dry.
2. Wipe away haze with a soft cloth.
3. Seal with grout sealer.

Tips:
• Before sealing, turn the ball over slowly to check for loose pieces or missing grout. Reattach any piece that is loose by removing the piece. Clear away any excess grout, apply adhesive to the piece, and put in place. Regrout as needed.

• Use a toothpick to go over each piece of tesserae to make sure that it has been cleaned of grout and adhesive. If there is any leftover glue, remove it with a razor blade.

• Let the ball dry for 72 hours before sealing. Do not place your ball outside without sealing it. To seal, fill a small spray bottle halfway with the tile sealer. Spray the whole ball, making sure all of the grout has been soaked. Wipe off the glass and let the ball dry. Now it is ready to be displayed inside or out. ❑

GLASS FLOWERS GAZING BALL

Designed by Robyn Huber

*"Gazing balls are a lot of fun because they look different in different types of lighting,"
says Robin. "I wanted to try some different designs with the bowling ball surface, so I
thought about big colorful flowers. I made sure that the bottom was empty of design
since it would be covered by the stand. I used black glass to fill in and black grout to
make the flowers stand out."*

SUPPLIES

Used bowling ball
Stained glass pieces, in various
   harmonizing color groups and black
Flatbacked glass marbles for flower
   centers
Plastic or wood putty
Clear silicone glue
Sanded grout - black
Old towel
Light colored crayon or china marker
Basic tools & supplies

INSTRUCTIONS

See the "Tips" section with the instructions for the Glass Triangles Gazing Ball.
Prepare:
1. Clean bowling ball well with soap and water. Fill the holes either with plastic or wood putty. Allow a couple of days for the putty to dry thoroughly.
2. Cut glass in triangles. (They do not have to be perfect!) The pieces should not be any bigger than 1-1/2" on a side.
3. Group pieces according to color family.
4. Sketch the design on the ball with a light colored crayon or china marker.

Attach Tesserae:
1. Set your ball on a bunched up towel to keep it from rolling as you work.
2. Glue glass marbles for flower centers.
3. Glue glass triangles to ball to form petals, using clear silicone glue. Place pieces no more than 1/2" apart. Be careful not to apply too much adhesive. Let each flower dry thoroughly before going on to the next one.

Grout:
1. Mix grout. Spread over tesserae. Wipe off excess. Let dry.
2. Wipe away haze with a soft cloth.
3. Seal with grout sealer. ❑

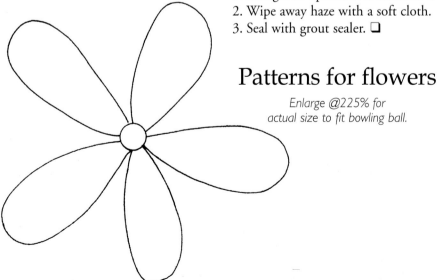

Patterns for flowers

*Enlarge @225% for
actual size to fit bowling ball.*

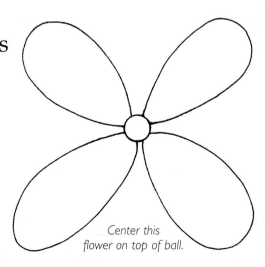

*Center this
flower on top of ball.*

MIRRORED DIAMONDS GAZING BALL

Designed by Robyn Huber

"The geometric design was fun to create with mirror and glass tiles," says Robyn. "I used tiles to sub-divide the ball into sections and filled each section with mirror and colored glass. This is Connie's favorite and now resides in her garden!"

SUPPLIES

Used bowling ball
Glass and mirror tiles, in various
    harmonizing color groups and black
Plastic or wood putty
Clear silicone glue
Sanded grout - black
Old towel
Light colored crayon or china marker
Basic tools & supplies

INSTRUCTIONS

See the "Tips" section with the instructions for the Glass Triangles Gazing Ball.

Prepare:
1. Clean bowling ball well with soap and water. Fill the holes either with plastic or wood putty. Allow a couple of days for the putty to dry thoroughly.
2. Cut glass 3/8" squares for the dividing bands and the glass diamonds. (They do not have to be perfect!)
3. Nip black glass and colored glass into irregular pieces.
4. Group pieces according to color family.
5. Sketch the design on the ball with a light colored crayon or china marker, using photo as a guide.

Attach Tesserae:
1. Set your ball on a bunched up towel to keep it from rolling as you work.
2. Glue glass squares to form bands.
3. Glue glass squares to form diamond shapes, using clear silicone glue. Place pieces no more than 1/2" apart. Be careful not to apply too much adhesive. If the adhesive gets on the top side of the glass, wipe it off immediately. Let each flower dry thoroughly before going on to the next one.
4. Glue mirror squares to connect diamonds.
5. Fill in areas around bands and diamonds with glass pieces. Let dry.

Grout:
1. Mix grout. Spread over tesserae. Wipe off excess. Let dry.
2. Wipe away haze with a soft cloth.
3. Seal with grout sealer. ❏

FRIENDLY FROG GARDEN STATUE

Although I was never a fan of little squirmy critters as a little girl (nor as a big girl, as far as that goes), I never met a froggie I didn't like. When I saw this frog I knew he was just right for the garden, and I also thought how perfect he would be near a pond. His big black eyes will wink when you pass by – as all creative folks and children know. Put your frog in a very special place. He has magical qualities and may hop away if you aren't watching and end up in a neighbor's yard!

SUPPLIES

Cement frog, 6-1/4" tall, 6-1/4" wide,
   10" long from head to back legs
Flatbacked marbles, 1" - 6 dark green,
   4 light green, 5 cat's eye green,
   4 jade green, 2 black (for the eyes)
50 green tiles, 3/4"
Mirror tiles, 1/2" - 6 peridot green,
   6 amber gold
25-30 pieces of nipped china
Sanded grout - green
Indoor/outdoor acrylic paint - green
1/2" paint brush
Clear silicone glue
Basic supplies & tools

INSTRUCTIONS

Prepare:
1. Nip the green tiles into many different sizes and shapes.
2. Nip some china floral pieces for accent on back of froggie.
3. Nip some of the amber mirror tiles in different sizes.

Attach Tesserae:
1. Glue the black marbles for the froggie's eyes.
2. Glue all the different colors of green marbles on the froggie's back.
3. Glue pieces of colored mirror tiles and china to fill in the rest of the back.
4. Cover the rest of the frog with the green tiles.

Grout:
1. Mix grout. Spread over tesserae. Wipe away excess. Let dry.
2. Wipe away haze with a soft cloth.
3. Seal grout.

Finish:
Paint the base of the froggie with green indoor/outdoor paint.

Tip:
• You can use china pieces left over from the Frog Crossing Stepping Stone or substitute some pretty blue and pink patterned china. ❑

MELLOW MUSHROOMS GARDEN STATUE

Mushrooms! I love them! When I saw these cement mushrooms at a garden center I could hardly wait to begin working on them. They reminded me of all the mushrooms I used to handpaint on everything in the 1970s. I even painted mushrooms on my friend Jim's refrigerator – those were the days, my friends. My VW bus was the only one at Woodstock with mushrooms painted on it, here and there, for just the right embellishment! Jim Stiles, who lives in New York City now, has some of my watercolor mushrooms hanging on his bedroom wall. They say if we live long enough everything comes back. What a treat to give Jim more of my hand created mushrooms! Life is good.

SUPPLIES

Cement mushroom statue, 9" tall,
   6-1/2" wide
12 round ceramic tiles, 1/2" and 1"
1 green paisley china cup
1 blue paisley china cup
4 orange tiles, 3/4"
3 glass butterflies (turquoise, cobalt
   and gold), 1"
1 brown-toned piece of chipped pottery
Indoor/outdoor paint - dark green
Acrylic craft paint - neon green
Sanded grout - white
Clear silicone adhesive
Basic tools & supplies

INSTRUCTIONS

Prepare:
1. Nip lots of china for the mushroom caps.
2. Nip brown-toned pottery for the stem.
3. Nip the orange tiles for the top of one of the smaller mushrooms.

Attach Tesserae:
1. Cover the mushroom caps with the tile and china pieces. If you have a lazy Susan, use it.
2. Glue pottery and china pieces on the stems. Let dry.
3. Turn statue upside down to glue pieces underneath the mushrooms. Let dry. Turn right side up.
4. Glue the glass butterflies in place. Let dry.

Grout:
1. Mix grout and tint with neon green paint.
2. Spread over tesserae. Wipe away excess. Let dry.
3. Wipe away haze with a soft cloth.

Finish:
1. Paint base of mushroom with neon green.
2. Dry brush base with deep green for a shaded look.
3. Seal grout. ❏

SNAIL PLANT POKE & GARDEN STATUE

Garden Statue

Sitting in the sun, this snail reflects its sparkling personality and reminds me why it jumped out at me when I saw it sitting "naked" on the shelf! Honestly, you will smile every time you pass it in your garden.

SUPPLIES

Snail garden statue, 10" long from
   head to tail, 6" high
Sparkling glass button for peak of
   snail shell, 1"
200 silver embossed mirror tiles, 1/2"
25 copper metallic glass tiles, 1"
15 gold metallic lime color glass tiles, 1"
2 amber Austrian crystals, 4mm
Gold metallic wax
Sanded grout - grout
Adhesive
Basic tools & supplies

INSTRUCTIONS

Prepare:
Nip the glass tiles and mirrors into quarters. You may have to nip some of these pieces even smaller as you begin to glue on the tiles.

Attach Tesserae:
1. Starting with the tip of the shell, work the silver and copper pieces into swirls of color.
2. Use the copper tiles for the back of the neck.
3. Use the lime tiles for the belly.
4. Glue the glass button at the center of the shell.
5. Glue the amber Austrian crystals on either side of the head for the eyes.

Grout:
1. Mix grout. Spread over tesserae. Wipe away excess. Let dry.
2. Wipe away haze with a soft cloth.

Finish:
Rub gold wax on the edge of the shell and the antennae to embellish. ❑

SNAIL PLANT POKE

Pictured on page 103

Here's the perfect plant poke to place near your snail statue. I love these plant pokes — they look great anywhere and take so little time to make. Watch out — it's hard to make just one! I've included a pattern for cutting your own plant poke from 3/4" thick wood.

SUPPLIES

Wooden plant poke, 3-1/4" tall, 5-1/4" wide
Snail ceramic tile, 2" square
12 pieces blue patterned china
7 pieces floral patterned china
35 pieces yellow and beige patterned china
2 acrylic stones - 1 butterfly, 1 "joy"
Sanded grout - terra cotta
Indoor/outdoor paint - terra cotta
Adhesive
Basic tools & supplies

INSTRUCTIONS

Prepare:
Nip the china into appropriate-sized pieces.

Attach Tesserae:
1. Glue the snail tile in the middle of the plant poke.
2. Glue the two stone pieces in place.
3. Glue the blue china pieces along the bottom.
4. Glue a row of the floral china pieces above the blue ones.
5. Fill in the rest of the space with the yellow and beige patterned china.

Grout:
1. Mix grout. Spread over tesserae. Wipe away excess. Let dry.
2. Wipe away haze with a soft cloth.
3. Seal grout.

Finish:
Paint exposed wood with terra cotta paint. ❏

Pattern for Plant Poke

Cut from 3/4" thick wood.

BEAUTY AT THE DOOR DOOR STOP

It's just the thing for keeping the porch door propped open. I used some ornate metal pieces (one was a drawer pull), some small square tiles in a variety of colors, and a pretty painted tile. Some of the tiles were grouted; others weren't.

SUPPLIES

Surface: cement door stop or brick
2 ornamental metal pieces
1 decorative tile with painted design
Square tiles - some rose, some blue,
  plus assorted colors
Sanded grout - buttercream
Adhesive of your choice
Basic tools & supplies

INSTRUCTIONS

Attach Tesserae:
1. Glue ornamental metal pieces in place.
2. Glue decorative tile in place.
3. Fill in around decorative tile with small square tiles, staggering the placement like courses of bricks. Nip tiles as needed to keep pattern.
4. Glue a row of rose tiles across the top.
5. Glue a row of blue tiles across the bottom. Let dry.

Grout:
1. Mix grout. Spread over center section of tiles. Wipe away excess. Let dry.
2. Wipe away haze with a soft cloth. ❏

SLEEPING KITTY

When I saw this cat lying on the floor looking so content, I envisioned a cat with a coat of many colors. This piece also would look great on the hearth of a fireplace or holding open a bedroom door.

SUPPLIES

Cement cat statue, 15" head to tail, 11" front to back

Broken 4" x 4" tiles - red, orange, yellow, light blue, turquoise blue

1 red glass heart

5 kinds of broken china pieces to match the solid colors

2 black tiles, 3/4" (for eyes)

6 pink tiles, 3/4" (for inside ears and nose)

Sanded grout - purple

Clear silicone adhesive

Basic tools & supplies

INSTRUCTIONS

Preparation:

1. Nip color tiles into many small pieces.
2. Nip 5 different piles of china into small pieces.
3. Nip black tiles for the eyes and pink tiles for the ears and nose.
4. Using a pencil mark off the cat into sections to fill in with the tiles and china.

Attach Tesserae:

1. Glue on the eyes, nose, and ears.
2. Glue in the solid colors and the red heart.
3. Fill in the alternating spaces with coordinating color patterned china. You may want to choose to do a striped tail, alternating solid tiles and patterned china.
4. Allow to dry overnight.

Grout:

1. Mix grout and spread over a section at a time, making sure you get the grout into every opening. By the time you have grouted the entire piece, you will be able to go back to the starting place and begin wiping off the excess grout with dry sponge. Let dry.
2. Wipe away haze with a soft cloth.

Finish:

If your cat is going to be used outside, seal the grout with several coats of grout sealer. Allow it to dry 24-48 hours before putting it outside. ❑

"WELCOMMEN" WOODEN SHOE

One day my husband Ken and I were shopping, and while he was in a convenience store getting money from a teller machine, I spotted a little antiques store across from where we were parked. A pair of wooden shoes was in the window with silk tulips in them for display. I could see those shoes covered with blue and white tiles and china, filled with yellow tulips every spring to welcome visitors to my front door. By the time Ken came out with money in his hand, I was out of the car asking him to tag along. What a patient man! I bought the pair – one for me and one for a gift.

SUPPLIES

1 wooden shoe - 12" long,
   3-3/4" wide
2 blue and white patterned china
   dinner plates
1 blue china plate, 6-7" in diameter
40 royal blue tiles, 3/4"
1 two-toned round blue tile, 3/4"
Sanded grout - white
Adhesive
Basic tools & supplies

INSTRUCTIONS

Prepare:
1. Nip the blue and white patterned china.
2. Nip the blue china plate into pieces 3/8" to 1/2".
3. Nip royal blue tiles in quarters. Nip some in smaller pieces.

Attach Tesserae:
1. Glue royal blue tile pieces on the toe and turned up bottom of the shoe.
2. Make a 1" border of dark blue tile pieces, bringing them into a triangle at the top front of the shoe.
3. Glue the round tile at the point of the triangle.
4. Fill in the rest of the area with nipped china pieces.

Grout:
1. Mix grout. Spread over tesserae. Remove excess. Let dry.
2. Wipe away haze with a soft cloth.
3. Seal grout.

Tip:
• If you plan to use this piece to hold a plant or tulip bulbs, seal the inside of the wooden shoe with wood sealer. Add a plastic liner before planting. ❏

Mosaic
Pots
&
Planters

Terra cotta pots and planters are ideal surfaces for mosaics. An additional benefit is that the mosaic further insulates the pot, protecting the plant's soil from drying out. Wooden window boxes and planters are easy-to-work with flat surfaces. You'll find all sorts of surfaces at garden centers and home improvement stores.

Pictured at right: Eggshell Clay Pot

EGGSHELL CLAY POT

Carla D'Iorio came up with this quickie that uses eggshells for a mosaic look. Carla was making an omelet for a large family gathering and decided to save all those eggshells. She shared her idea with me, and together we came up with a design. This is a project where you can have your kids work along with you. So start cracking those eggs!

SUPPLIES

5" terra cotta pot
4 light blue tiles, 3/4"
4 cobalt blue tiles, 3/4"
4 orange tiles, 3/4"
16 orange tiles, 3/8"
16 yellow tiles, 3/8"
2 oz. of china pieces in complementary colors

2-3 eggshells
Gold metallic wax
Paint brushes (one to use for applying glue)
Brush-on laminating liquid
Sanded grout - blue
Basic tools & supplies

INSTRUCTIONS

Prepare:
Using the nippers, cut fairly small pieces of china (3/8" to 1/2").

Attach Tesserae on Rim:
1. Using the photo as a guide, glue the 3/4" tiles, alternating colors.
2. Glue on the 3/8" tiles.
3. Fill in the empty spaces with the china pieces.

Grout:
1. Mix grout according to general instructions and grout the rim. Allow to dry.
2. Seal with a grout sealer.

Finish:
1. Using a paste brush, working on one small area at a time, paint on a thin coat of glue. Take half an eggshell and press it right on the glue, allowing the pattern to form however the shell cracks. Continue until the entire lower part of the pot is covered with shells. Let glue dry.
2. Using your finger, rub some gold metallic wax on the shells, letting some of the white to show through. Allow to dry overnight.
3. Using a paintbrush, coat the shells with brush-on laminating liquid to seal them. ❏

Pictured left to right: Glass Circles Pot, Hearts & Flowers Pot, Eggshell Pot.

GLASS CIRCLES POT

Pictured on page 111

I was looking at some polymer cane pieces and decided they would make very interesting tiles for a pot. Black tiles and purple grout make them stand out.

SUPPLIES

5" white ceramic flower pot
15 pieces polymer cane
Tile pieces - black and other dark colors
Tiles, 3/8" in white and bright colors
Sanded grout - purple
Clear silicone adhesive
Basic tools & supplies

INSTRUCTIONS

Prepare:
1. Slice 1/4" tiles from the polymer canes. Bake according to package instructions.
2. Nip the 3/8 tiles in half.
3. Nip dark colored tiles as needed into small pieces of all sizes and shapes.

Attach Tesserae:
1. Glue a band of brightly colored tiles just below the rim.
2. Glue the polymer tiles in place, using photo as a guide.
3. Fill in around them with pieces of dark colored tile. Let dry.

Grout:
1. Mix grout. Spread over tesserae. Remove excess. Let dry.
2. Wipe away haze with a soft cloth.
3. Seal grout. ❏

HEARTS & FLOWERS POT

Pictured on page 111

Heart-shaped tiles were the inspiration for this pot.

SUPPLIES

6" terra cotta pot
12 heart-shaped tiles, various colors
Pieces of floral patterned china
A few small tiles in bright colors
Pieces of broken terra cotta pots
Sanded grout - blue gray
Clear silicone adhesive
Basic tools & supplies

INSTRUCTIONS

Prepare:
1. Nip six of the heart-shaped tiles in half to form the leaves.
2. Nip the tiles, china, and terra cotta as needed into small pieces of all sizes and shapes.

Attach Tesserae:
1. Glue heart-shaped tiles and "leaves" to rim of pot, using photo as a guide.
2. Fill in around them with pieces of china and colored tiles.
3. Glue pieces of terra cotta around the rest of the pot. Let dry.

Grout:
1. Mix grout. Spread over tesserae. Remove excess. Let dry.
2. Wipe away haze with a soft cloth.
3. Seal grout. ❏

STRAWBERRY POT

I love this piece and I had so much fun making it. I thought about all the fun and different plants you can put in a strawberry pot. I wanted the mosaic part of it to go with any plant, any color, and it does. I used bits and pieces of lots of things and a few handmade word tiles that were designed by Kat Kirby, a friend and marvelous potter. This design reminds me of a crazy quilt. It's a good piece for using up odds and ends of tiles and china from other projects. Let your imagination run wild.

Terra cotta strawberry pot - 12" tall, 7" diameter at top
2 lb. tiles in assorted shapes
China in assorted patterns or 1 lb. nipped china
1/2 lb. flat backed marbles
7 china cups
6 pottery word tiles
25 patterned mirror tiles
Sanded grout - terra cotta
2 bricks
Old bath towel
Clear silicone adhesive
Basic tools & supplies

INSTRUCTIONS

Prepare:
1. Nip china if you aren't using pre-nipped china.
2. Nip the handles off the china cups and nip the cups into pieces. (The curved parts of the cups work nicely on the pot's rounded surface.)
3. Lay the pot on its side on a towel for protective padding. Use a brick or other heavy object on either side to keep it from rolling.

Attach Tesserae:
Glue tiles and china pieces, working on one small section at a time, starting from the top and working down to the bottom of the jar. Mix the colors, sizes, and shapes as you work for a random, interesting look. Allow each section to dry thoroughly before turning and working on the next section. Continue until the entire piece is covered.

Grout:
1. Stand the pot on end. Mix grout. Spread over tesserae. Remove excess. Keep turning the pot until you have covered the entire pot. Allow grout to dry thoroughly.
2. Wipe away haze with a soft cloth.
3. Seal grout.

Tip:
• If you have a turntable or lazy Susan, it is a great way to grout the piece – you can keep moving the turntable during the grouting process. ❏

HEARTS & ROSES PLANTER

Designed by Carla D'Iorio and Connie Sheerin

I love the feeling of love and romance that this design evokes. Carla came up with the idea of using the back of a plate to create the outline of the heart, and we worked on this one together. The same technique could be used to create an outline for any shape. What a great way to use the part of the plate that we usually toss away!

SUPPLIES

Rectangular wooden planter with a design area 16-1/4" x 4-3/4"

11 leaf-shaped tiles in shades of green - 1 large (1-1/2"), 4 medium (1-1/4"), and 6 small (7/8")

1 china dinner plate with a rose pattern and a scalloped, gold-trimmed edge

2 china cups with a rose pattern and gold flecked handles

1 rose colored china saucer

20 light pink tiles, 3/4"

Indoor/outdoor paint - gold metallic, rose

1/2" paintbrush

Adhesive of your choice

Basic tools & supplies

INSTRUCTIONS

Prepare:

1. Nip the handles off the china cups and save to use as accent pieces.

2. Using the china nippers, nip out the rose designs from the china cups and plate.

3. Nip the scalloped edge of the plate, making each scallop a china tile.

4. Cut the pink tiles in half to use as edging.

5. Nip the rose saucer in pieces to use as filler.

6. Nip the darker rose under the rim of the plate and the base to use as the outline of the heart.

Attach Tesserae:

1. Glue on the heart outline.

2. Fill the center of the outline with rose patterned pieces of china. (You will notice I chose to add a couple pieces of the gold cup handle within the same space.)

3. Glue the scalloped gold trimmed pieces across the top.

4. Glue the halves of the light pink tiles along the bottom and under the scal-

loped china pieces.

5. Place 6-8 scattered roses in the space remaining.

6. Glue leaves to accent your smaller roses, using photo as a guide for placement.

7. Glue more broken cup handle pieces.

8. Glue the darker rose china pieces to fill in.

Grout:

1. Mix white grout with small drops of the rose paint to tint it a light shade of pink. Apply grout. Remove excess. Let dry.

2. Seal the grout well – this piece will get water splashed on it every time you water your flowers.

Paint:

1. Paint the ends and back of the planter with rose.

2. Paint the top of the handles of the box with metallic gold to bring out the gold on the scalloped pieces and

TURTLE GARDEN STATUE

Pictured on page 117

I found this turtle on a visit to Newport, Rhode Island. (I had great hopes of finding a hare, but no such luck!) This friendly little fellow now resides next to the umbrella stand in my foyer. I brought him inside so I could see him more often than I would if he lived in my garden. I find I have grown very fond of my mosaic critters! (I used one china cup to make this turtle, but a saucer would work as well.)

SUPPLIES

Cement turtle, 8" long, 5" wide

35 tiles of various colors, 3/8"

20 round tiles of various colors

1 turquoise china cup with Chinese motifs

Sanded grout - green

China nippers

Basic tools & supplies

INSTRUCTIONS

Prepare:

Nip the china cup into pieces.

Attach Tesserae:

1. Glue the 3/8" tiles in place, alternating colors around the rim of the turtle shell.

2. Glue the round tiles over the back of the turtle.

3. Fill in around the circle tiles with the china pieces.

Grout:

1. Mix grout.

2. Apply to the back of the turtle, being careful not to get it on the rest of the turtle. If you do, wipe it off immediately with a damp cloth, as the grout will stain. Let dry.

3. Wipe away haze with a soft cloth.

4. Seal the grout if you plan to use your turtle outdoors. ❑

PLANT POKES

Who doesn't like these adorable plant pokes? I found these precious tiles with embossed critters. Can't you just see them poking out of your garden by the pond or in a pot of cactus on the deck? They are fun, fast projects!

Dragonfly Plant Poke

SUPPLIES

Wooden plant poke, 4-1/2" tall,
  3-1/4" wide
Dragonfly tile, 2" square
Green glass tile, 3" square
1 small floral motif china plate
Sanded grout - denim blue
Indoor/outdoor acrylic paint -
  denim blue
Small paintbrush
Adhesive
Basic tools & supplies

INSTRUCTIONS

Prepare:
1. Nip just enough china to trim the edge.
2. Nip glass tile to fill in between the dragonfly tile and the china.

Attach Tesserae:
1. Glue the dragonfly tile in the center of the poke.
2. Glue the china floral tiles around the outer edge.
3. Fill in with the green glass pieces.

Grout:
1. Mix grout. Spread over tesserae. Wipe away excess. Let dry.
2. Wipe away haze with a soft cloth.
3. Seal grout.

Finish:
Paint exposed wood with denim blue paint. ❑

Tortoise Plant Poke

SUPPLIES

Half-circle shaped plant poke with
  rippled edge, 3-1/2" tall, 5-1/4" wide
Tortoise tile, 2" square
6 circle tiles, 1/2"
1 circle tile, 1"
2 gold iridescent glass butterflies, 1"
2 green iridescent glass butterflies, 1"
12 tiles in assorted colors, 3/8"
12 assorted floral print china pieces, 3/8"
Indoor/outdoor paint - mint green
Small paint brush
Sanded grout - seafoam green
Adhesive
Basic tools & supplies

INSTRUCTIONS

Attach Tesserae:
1. Glue the tortoise tile in the center of the poke.
2. Glue the circle tiles on the outer edge. Glue a couple in the inner space.
3. Glue the glass butterflies, using photo as a guide for placement.
4. Fill in the area, alternating the china and tile pieces. You may have to nip some smaller pieces. Let dry.

Grout:
1. Mix grout. Spread over tesserae. Wipe away excess. Let dry.
2. Wipe away haze with a soft cloth.
3. Seal grout.

Finish:
Paint exposed wood with mint green paint. Let dry. ❑

TRES PAPILLION PLANTER

I love color. Most of my mosaics aren't subtle, but occasionally I use pastel colors. This time my inspiration was the wrapping paper from a birthday gift. The images looked like they had been hand painted with watercolors. I remembered some great prints I had that I could use to the ends. I knew I wanted it to stay airy, so the last element I thought to use was paper doilies. I have to laugh when I think how that wrapping paper was the starting point. It pays to see everything as a possibility!

SUPPLIES

Wooden planter with front panel measuring 10-1/4" x 3-5/8"

4 pastel colored heart-shaped tiles

25 white 3/4" tiles

1 each pastel yellow, baby blue, pink, and mint green tiles, 3/4"

White paper doilies

Gift wrap with butterfly motifs (or paint your own!)

Multi-colored metallic foil

Foil adhesive

White craft glue

Paste brush

Copper tape, 1/4" wide

6 clear glass pieces, 2" square, 1/8" thick

Acrylic craft paints - seafoam green, marigold yellow

Brush-on laminating liquid

1/2" paint brush

1" paint brush

Sandpaper, 220 grit

Decoupage scissors

Sanded grout - buttercream

Nylon kitchen pot scrubber

Adhesive of your choice

Basic tools & supplies

INSTRUCTIONS

Prepare:
Cut the 3/4" tiles into small pieces of different sizes and shapes.

Make Glass Sandwich Tiles:
See "How to Make Glass Sandwich Tiles" in the Basic Techniques section.
1. Brush foil adhesive on 3 of the 2" glass squares. Allow to dry until clear but still tacky.
2. Place foil pieces on the adhesive, using several colors for a rainbow look. Brush off excess with a nylon kitchen scrubber, rubbing lightly.
3. Place the paper doily on the foil, trim as needed to fit, and glue to the metallic background.
4. Cut out the butterflies and glue one on top of each doily.
5. Allow the tiles to dry overnight so all of the glue is thoroughly dry so no moisture will be trapped into the glass sandwich.
6. Place the second piece of glass on top.
7. Seal the edges with foil tape.

Attach Tesserae:
1. Using a ruler, mark the placement of the glass tiles.
2. Glue the glass tiles to the front panel of the planter.
3. Glue a pastel heart in each corner.
4. Fill in with white tiles, starting with the outside borders. Add different colored pastel tile pieces here and there for accents. Let dry.

Grout:
1. Mix a seafoam green grout, which is achieved by adding some green paint to buttercream grout. (It will dry a few shades lighter than the paint.)
2. Apply grout to tiled side of planter. Let dry.

Finish:
1. Sand the wood that isn't covered by tesserae. Wipe away dust with a tack cloth.
2. Paint the planter except the ends and inside with seafoam green.
3. Paint the ends and inside with marigold yellow.
4. Cut out some motifs from the gift wrap for the ends of the box.
5. Glue to box with white glue, making sure you remove all air bubbles. Allow to dry completely.
6. Apply a coat of brush-on laminating liquid to seal the wood, inside and out. This will help protect your paint. Let dry.

Tip:
• Even though you have sealed the wood, it is a good idea to insert a plastic liner before placing flower pots in the planter. ❑

Mosaic
Projects
for
Outdoor
Friends

Bird baths, birdhouses, bird feeders, and butterfly houses are beautiful additions to any back yard and wonderful surfaces for creating mosaics. Flying creatures will be attracted to the bright colors and sparkle. You will, too!

Pictured at right: Sunshine Bird Bath.

Sunshine Bird Bath

Pictured on page 121

When I spotted this birdbath, I yelled with glee so loudly that I think I scared shoppers for several aisles. (My husband, who is getting used to these sorts of reactions, nonchalantly followed the sound. He smiled, knowing that there had to be something more wonderful than he could see.)
It was different and like none other I had ever seen, not to mention that it is lightweight and the top comes off. I had been saving that round sun tile for something very special, and this was it! You will love matching the colors and working around the colors in your centerpiece tile.

Supplies

Wrought iron birdbath, 3 ft. high with a 16" wide bowl
52 royal blue tiles, 3/4"
36 yellow tiles, 3/4"
6 iridescent gold glass stars, 3/4"
6 iridescent blue glass stars, 3/4"
Round sun handpainted tile, 4-1/4"
18 round tiles, various sizes and colors
8 flatbacked marbles, various colors
14 yellow tiles, 3/8"
14 gold ochre tiles, 3/8"
Broken pieces from a brown and gold patterned piece of pottery or china
Broken pieces from a goldish tan piece of pottery or china
Sanded grout - dark blue
Adhesive
Basic tools & supplies

Instructions

Preparation:
1. Nip all the pottery pieces so once you start gluing you can just continue working the design.
2. Cut the yellow 3/4" tiles in half.

Attach Tesserae:
1. Glue the round tile in the center.
2. Glue the yellow and gold ochre 3/8" square tiles, alternating the two colors around the center tile.
3. Glue the royal blue tiles around the outside edge. Glue the yellow half tiles in a second row under the blue.
4. Place the stars and marbles in the open space, scattering them in an attractive way.
5. Fill in with the broken pieces of pottery. Let the dry 24 hours.

Grout:
1. Mix grout and apply from the center out to the rim.
2. Let dry for about 15 minutes. Wipe with sponge.
3. Let dry for another 15 minutes. Wipe again and buff the tiles with a soft cloth.

Finish:
Seal with grout sealer, following the manufacturer's instructions. Let dry 24 hours before filling with water. ❏

BLUE TRIANGLES BIRDHOUSE

Designed by Robyn Huber

"This birdhouse had a cute heart shaped opening so I decided to use heart-shaped glass accents," says Robyn. Because she also loves blue glass, she created a blue roof and put blue glass and blue mirror on the walls. The mirror is very beautiful in the sunshine as the light dances off reflections of blue.

SUPPLIES

Wooden birdhouse with heart-shaped opening
Stained glass - blue, purple, aqua
Mirror squares
3 iridescent glass hearts
Sanded grout - purple
Clear silicone glue
Indoor/outdoor acrylic paint - purple
Basic tools & supplies

INSTRUCTIONS

Prepare:
1. Cut 3/4" glass and mirror squares for the roof. (They do not have to be perfect!)
2. Cut remaining blue and purple glass pieces into irregular triangle shapes.

Attach Tesserae:
1. Glue heart shaped glass pieces in a row under the opening.
2. Glue irregular triangle-shaped pieces to the sides of the house. Place pieces no more than 1/2" apart. (They can be as close as you want.) Fill in all space on one side before moving to another side.
3. Glue square glass and mirror tiles to roof.

Grout:
1. Mix grout. Spread over tesserae on roof. Wipe away excess. Let dry.
2. Spread grout over tesserae on sides, working one side at a time. Wipe away excess. Let dry.

3. Wipe away haze with a soft cloth.

Finish:
1 Paint openings and edges of roof with purple paint. Let dry 72 hours.
2. Seal grout.

Tips:
• You do not have to glue glass on every side of the house. You can paint some of the sides or maybe the roof instead of creating a mosaic.

• Be careful not to apply too much adhesive. If the adhesive gets on the top side of the glass, wipe it off immediately. Remove excess dry glue with a razor blade. ❑

FEED THE BIRDS BIRD FEEDER

Designed by Dolly Clark

Dolly wanted to make something with mosaics for her parents' shore house, and this is her very first mosaic. I hope it encourages those of you who are just beginning. Choose paint colors that complement the mosaic part of the birdhouse – it really doesn't matter what colors you choose, as anything matches the outdoors! Be sure to hang it so you can see it through a window in your home.

SUPPLIES

Wooden bird feeder, 6" wide, 10" high, with 7" square base
1-1/2 lbs. tiles in various colors, 3/8"
15 flatbacked marbles in various colors
30 various shells, including mini sand dollars, a seahorse, and a starfish
Indoor/outdoor paints - mint green, pink, baby blue, yellow
1/2" paint brush
Sanded grout - buttercream
Brush-on laminating liquid
Optional: Sea sponge

INSTRUCTIONS

Attach Tesserae:
1. Outline the roof with 3/8" tiles.
2. Place flatbacked marbles and seashells in a scattered pattern on all surfaces.
3. Fill in the rest of the area with the 3/8" tiles.

Grout:
1. Mix grout and apply according to general instructions.
2. Seal grout.

Finish:
1. Paint the exposed wooden areas in pastel colors. Let dry. *Option:* Sponge the base with layers of color as shown in the photo. Let dry between layers.
2. Seal paint with brush-on laminating liquid.
3. Glue a few sea findings on the painted part of the birdhouse to embellish. ❑

FLOWER GARDEN BUTTERFLY HOUSE

Designed by Robyn Huber

Says Robyn, "Connie wanted to use fun flower and butterfly glass shapes as accents. I thought the yellow, orange and reds would create a cheerful look." Bright colors attract butterflies, too.

SUPPLIES

Wooden butterfly house
Stained glass - red, yellow, orange,
    green, aqua
Mirror squares
18 glass flowers in various colors
18 glass butterflies in various colors
Sanded grout - white, dark brown
Clear silicone glue
Indoor/outdoor acrylic paint - orange, red
Basic tools & supplies

INSTRUCTIONS

Prepare:
1. Cut 3/4" glass and mirror squares for the roof. (They do not have to be perfect!)
2. Cut remaining red, yellow, and orange glass pieces into irregular triangle shapes.
3. Cut green and aqua glass pieces into strips to use as flower leaves and stems.

Attach Tesserae:
1. Glue the leaf and stem pieces along the base of the house.
2. Glue the flowers in place.
3. Glue butterflies to the sides of the house, using photo as a guide for placement.
4. Glue square glass and mirror tiles to roof.
5. Glue irregular triangle-shaped pieces to the sides of the house. Place pieces no more than 1/2" apart. (They can be as close as you want.) Fill in all space on one side before moving to another side.

Grout:
1. Mix brown grout. Spread over tesserae

on roof. Wipe away excess. Let dry.
2. Mix white grout. Spread over tesserae, working one side at a time. Wipe away excess. Let dry.
3. Wipe away haze with a soft cloth.

Finish:
1. Paint openings on house with red paint.
2. Paint edges of roof with orange paint. Let dry 72 hours.
3. Seal grout. Let dry.

Tip:
• You do not have to glue glass on every side of the house. You can paint some of

METRIC CONVERSION CHART

Inches to Millimeters and Centimeters

Inches	MM	CM
1/8	3	.3
1/4	6	.6
3/8	10	1.0
1/2	13	1.3
5/8	16	1.6
3/4	19	1.9
7/8	22	2.2
1	25	2.5
1-1/4	32	3.2
1-1/2	38	3.8
1-3/4	44	4.4
2	51	5.1
3	76	7.6
4	102	10.2
5	127	12.7
6	152	15.2
7	178	17.8
8	203	20.3
9	229	22.9
10	254	25.4
11	279	27.9
12	305	30.5

Yards to Meters

Yards	Meters
1/8	.11
1/4	.23
3/8	.34
1/2	.46
5/8	.57
3/4	.69
7/8	.80
1	.91
2	1.83
3	2.74
4	3.66
5	4.57
6	5.49
7	6.40
8	7.32
9	8.23
10	9.14

INDEX

INDEX